BEYOND MAGA

From Trump's campaign slogan to political movement to restoring the Republic

Why the MAGA Movement arose, where it must go from here, and how MAGA can save America

DOC CONTRARIAN

Contents

For A Quick Read	v
Disclaimer and Essential Information	vii
Introduction	xi
1. The Origins Of The Maga Movement	1
2. But Is It Maga?	23
3. Maga, The Tea Party, And The Gop	33
4. Maga Enemies	43
5. 2024 Is Coming	63
6. Maga: 2024 And Beyond	75
7. Moving Beyond Maga	83
8. Bonus Chapter—The Sins Of Trump And The Big Steal	103
9. Afterward—The Red Speech	111
10. A Note on References	115
11. Appendix 1	117
12. Appendix 2	121
About the Author	125
Notes	129

For A Quick Read

Time is a precious and valuable commodity for all of us. Not everyone will have the time or inclination to read this book in its entirety. For those, I've made it possible to quickly grasp the essentials of the work in only a few minutes.

Each chapter begins with a pithy quote, followed by the summary, and then the chapter, in the following styles:

"Don't feel special. I trigger everybody."—Doc Contrarian

This is the summary, which boils each chapter down into an incredibly concise few sentences. Just read these chapter summaries if you are pressed for time, or only want to fake having read it at cocktail parties, state dinners or all-night bull sessions.

This is the chapter, wherein lies all the good stuff. The Author labored mightily over this verbiage, so the least you could do is appreciate it. Even if you didn't, tell all your friends that you **LOVED it and gave it a 5 star review on Amazon**. Insist that they rush out and buy their own copies and do the same, because 5 star reviews are to Amazon what money is to politics—lifeblood.

Disclaimer and Essential Information

"Giving money and power to government is like giving whiskey and car keys to teenage boys."—P. J. O'Rourke

This book is not intended to be a comprehensive statement about President Trump's policies, his positions on the issues, or a potential MAGA-centric platform. A wealth of information on these subjects already exists, and I have included transcripts or video links in the Appendices to some of those sources I feel are most useful on these subjects.

To understand the MAGA Movement I recommend starting with the Declaration of Independence and the Constitution, as they are the foundational documents of the nation.

Washington's Farewell Address and Jefferson's first Inaugural Address convey the distilled thinking of two of our nation's Founders and early leaders, and as such provide insights into the kind of government they envisioned for their new country.

Trump's *Great Again*, published in November 2015, is an excellent starting point for those seeking to understand his political philosophy from the vantage point of early in his first campaign. His 2015 campaign announcement, 2016 Inaugural Address and his 2020 RNC nomination acceptance speech are also invaluable for understanding what he wanted (and presumably still wants) to accomplish, and the 2020 RNC speech also lists some of the things he was most proud of doing for this nation. For President Trump's concerns and possible solutions to the country's ills prior to his Mar-a-Lago campaign announcement, I refer the reader to his 2022 America First and CPAC speeches. The President laid out his vision for the nation at his Mar-A-Lago campaign announcement, and since then has launched his campaign website (DonaldJTrump.com), as well as a Rumble channel, which he uses for video updates. He also frequently posts on Truth Social, despite having been recently restored to Twitter and Facebook. Given his history of being banned from Twitter and Facebook, as well as the rapid growth of Truth Social, it's unlikely that he will return to platforms that previously banned him.

President Trump's CPAC address on March 4, 2023 is perhaps the single best indicator of his immediate priorities when he is re-elected in 2024 (or, if you prefer, restored to the office that was fraudulently denied him).

Numerous sources are available which provide extensive coverage of the irregularities (and worse) that surround the 2020 Presidential election. Dr. Peter Navarro's three-part analysis[1] is probably the best introduction to the controversy and issues involved, for those who have been living under a rock since mid-2020. Mike Lindell's efforts, including starting his own platform, FrankSpeech.com, cannot be understated. Molly Hemingway's excellent ***Rigged: How***

the Media, Big Tech and the Democrats Seized Our Elections begins with an excellent summary of the Democrat's history of complaining about "stolen elections" that highlights the immediate pivot in the narrative that occurred in November 2020. Joe Hoft has covered the issue extensively at The Gateway Pundit, and his books ***The Steal*** (both first and second volumes) are also highly recommended. Finally, Patrick Colbeck's ***The 2020 Coup*** gives an eyewitness account of some of what went on in Detroit during and after the election, and is one of the best collections of evidence as well as a thoughtful consideration of the entire issue available. There are many others, but these provide a firm grounding in the facts—not the propaganda—about what really happened to deny Donald J. Trump a second consecutive term in office.

I've also provided a list of some of the other books that most influenced the creation of this work in the Appendices. Each is highly recommended, as every one will add to your appreciation of the wonder that is the MAGA Movement, our current perilous situation, and how we may move forward with the restoration of the Republic.

I have deliberately kept the number of specific references relatively low (well, it's what *I* consider "relatively low") because this is not intended to be a scholarly dissertation or scientific publication. The references I've included are those I consider necessary to document specific points. When excerpts from books are cited, the relevant chapter of the book is cited while pages rarely are given. This is due to the nature of eBooks, where alterations in font size alter the page numbers and counts. As most of my reading is done on Kindle for iOS due to poor eyesight, this is an unavoidable, mildly unfortunate sequela of an otherwise helpful technology.

I encourage readers to research my statements for themselves and reach their own conclusions. If you agree, fine; if not, that is your privilege and your right.

As I have said for years, you have the right to disagree with me. You absolutely have the God-given, Constitutionally-guaranteed right to be wrong!

Introduction

"Patriotism is supporting your country all the time and your government when it deserves it."—Mark Twain

What would the world be like if Donald J. Trump hadn't run for President in 2016? Which of the other Republican candidates could have beaten Hillary Clinton? Who else could have energized old-school Rust Belt Democrats, Blue Dogs, Reagan Democrats, Tea Party remnants, small-L libertarians, and Evangelicals across the nation like Donald J. Trump? Without Trump, we'd have President Hillary, First Spouse Bill, and for the Democrats the good times would have kept on rolling. As for the rest of us, we'd be lucky to be ignored while the heartland withered and died. Trump's grassroots-up strategy and campaign message resonated with millions of Americans who wanted the America Trump described—an America made great again. Those millions found their slogan—Make America Great Again—turned it into a symbol—MAGA—and rallied around it to put Trump into the White House. Now, after two years of the disastrous Biden regime, the MAGA movement continues to be a force to be reckoned with inside the Republican Party and across the country. Beyond MAGA is a call to action for those who believe in unalienable rights endowed by the Creator and a government established to secure those rights, empowered by the consent of the governed. It's for the millions of Americans who want to put America First, Make America Great Again, and keep it that way.

What might the world be like today if Donald John Trump hadn't run for President in 2016?

Think back to the 2016 Republican Presidential debates. Could any of those candidates have defeated Hillary Clinton in the general election? Who could have energized the Republican base and drawn in abandoned old-school Democrats in the Rust Belt? Who could have excited those Blue Dogs, Reagan Democrats, Tea Party remnants, small-L libertarians and Evangelicals across the nation? Which one would have inspired more enthusiastic grassroots support than any Republican since The Gipper himself?

One of them might have, but I doubt it.

Certainly not the candidate who was the Establishment's obvious choice for the nomination. When that candidate's team knew their guy was so excitement-free that adding an exclamation point to his logo seemed like a good idea? That wasn't just sad, it was a sign of a staff grasping at straws. It might as well have been an admission of defeat before the first vote was cast in November.

So, if the Orange Man hadn't ridden down that escalator in 2015… if he hadn't thrown his hat (and his very own, very real hair) into the ring…if he hadn't promised to Make America Great Again?

What kind of country would we be living in today?

Hillary Clinton would have been elected President and we would have had Bill back in the White House as First Spouse. What's-his-name would have been Vice President, not that anyone would have noticed a non-entity like him. Some of the worst excesses of the Obama years might have ebbed, but for the Clintons and their buds in the Democratic Party, the good times would have just kept on rolling.

And for the rest of us 'way out in Flyover Country? The best we could have hoped for was to be ignored by our betters on the coasts as the heartland continued to wither and die.

Or maybe not. Maybe that spark that drove the Founders to imagine a different path than being subjects of the British Crown wouldn't have been extinguished. Maybe local groups would have risen up to push back against the tide of Progressivism. Maybe, just maybe, it would have been enough to shove the pendulum back the other way.

Maybe the Republican Party would have found their gonads, grown a spine, decided to start acting like conservatives for a change, and actually fought back against the Democrat's destruction of America….

Okay, now that's going beyond hope and pleasant fiction into florid delusion and fantasy land. Forget that last bit about the Republican Party, 'cause we all know that wouldn't happen in a million years.

But the rest of it? Could small groups of conservative Patriots start a movement to resist eight years of toxic, kleptocratic Leftyism under President Hillary? Even better, could they have leveraged that resistance into a conservative resurgence?

Kurt Schlichter's ***The Conservative Insurgency*** is a wonderful work of fiction that provides a glimpse of a hopeful future in a world where no one person rose to successfully challenge Her in

2016. Subtitled *The Struggle To Take America Back, 2009–2041*, it's written as an oral history of the rise and ultimate triumph of constitutional conservatives over the progressives who were ascendent in 2008.

Schlichter's protagonist remarks in the Introduction:

> "This was not the story of a single "great man" who came along at just the moment his country needed him. There is no Washington, Lincoln, King, or even a Reagan whose biography I could use as a means to tell the story of the struggle. While many of the individuals who rose to prominence during this process were notable for their foresight, courage, and wisdom, in retrospect these leaders were largely fungible. **No one name comes to mind when we think about the last 30 years. (Emphasis added)**

> "This was not a top-down movement but one created, motivated, and executed from the bottom up…it was thousands, and then millions, of individuals whose decentralized actions changed the course of American history."

Schlichter's 2041 is a happy place indeed. Constitutional conservatives control all three branches of government and have finally done what Republicans have been teasing us with for decades. They've reduced the size and overreach of the federal government, dismantled the nanny state apparatus, returned all but the government's mandated powers to the States, and controlled the outrageous spending of the late 20th and early 21st centuries.

As I said, it's a work of fiction.

Fiction or not, **The Conservative Insurgency** is a book with much to offer modern conservatives. It describes a grassroots-up strategy —an "Insurgency", if you will—against a Progressive Establishment with seemingly all the advantages. And yet, it offers a realistic vision of just how such an overwhelming opponent could eventually be brought down. Progressivism is by its very nature unstable and self-contradictory, and in the book, conservatives learned to use its weaknesses against its proponents. Conservatives also learned to play to their own strengths, including those inherent in being underdogs. They learned to beat the Lefties at their own games and kept on doing it, over and over again. Then, once they started taking power, they actually did what they said they were going to do and replaced Progressive policies with conservative solutions. When these conservative solutions worked, Schlichter's insurgents doubled down and did the whole thing again. Rinse, wash, repeat; and in just a few decades they'd taken their country back.

I know—shocking! Conservatives putting conservative solutions in place and continuing to do so, without surrendering to the Left? Unheard of! But again, it's fiction.

It was implementing conservative solutions that solved problems instead of generating good feelings and more problems that led to the conservatives' ultimate success. It's enough to make one wonder if that might work in the real world.

Released in 2015, **The Conservative Insurgency** predates Trump's campaign and election. When it was written, few expected a strong candidate to emerge from the morass of the Republican Establishment, and those that did expected him or her to be quickly dragged back down. A transformative figure who would actually carry out conservative policies wouldn't be allowed the nomination, much less win the general election. From a novelist's perspective, a grassroots uprising is a reasonable starting point, even if the most recent attempt at such a thing—the Taxed Enough Already (TEA) Party—had all but gone the way of the Whigs.

Unlike what happened with the fictional grassroots conservatives of ***The Conservative Insurgency*** and the real-world Tea Party, candidate Trump took the stage and promised to Make America Great Again. Millions of Americans—those abandoned by the globalist policies of the last few Presidents, disgusted by the steady progress of liberal dogmas over traditional values, desperate for a return to fiscal sanity, or just fed up with the corruption inside the Washington Beltway—suddenly found someone who spoke to them, about the things they cared about.

Those millions, despite their differences, all wanted the America Trump described—an America returned to greatness. They yearned for an America standing proudly on the world stage, not by virtue of force or coercion, but leading by example, with malice towards none and charity to all. They remembered the days when American industry and know-how were unquestioned, before they were outsourced and globalized out of existence. They wanted peace, not endless, pointless wars draining American blood and treasure for no apparent purpose.

Those millions found a slogan that perfectly described what they wanted—to Make America Great Again—and turned it into a four-letter symbol—MAGA. They christened a Movement with that symbol, and made it their identifier and their brand.

Those millions of MAGA loyalists found enough common ground between themselves to put Donald Trump in the White House. They cheered his wins and ground their teeth as his opponents attacked him at every turn. Thousands showed up to protest a stolen election on January 6th, 2021 and show their continuing support for their President and the MAGA Movement, and many of them would end up being sent to a literal gulag for their trouble.

This book was written for those millions of Americans who consider themselves members of the Make America Great Again (MAGA) Movement. It's also for those who are curious about the Movement and have an open mind about its origins, basic ideas, and what it may become in the future. Ultimately, it was written for anyone who considers themselves to be a supporter of an America First agenda, or who is willing to embrace the ideas upon which the country was founded.

Donald J. Trump is a phenomenon, not a politician; that much was obvious from the first day of his campaign. Unlike the vast majority of politicians, President Trump aggressively worked to fulfill his campaign promises. This is just one of many things about him that continually baffled his opponents during his first term and terrifies them now. His style of deal-making—the blustering, the exaggerations, the seemingly off-the-wall statements, and other tactics calculated to throw his opponents off their game, combined with an ironclad determination to deliver once the deal is made—has arguably been more effective in politics than it was in the business world.

When Trump makes a promise to his MAGA supporters, they know that he'll try to make good on it. That makes his supporters love him all the more, and rightfully worries Establishment politicians and his other assorted enemies.

Donald J. Trump has been called narcissistic, egotistical, and self-aggrandizing. He's been accused of always seeking to present himself in the best possible light. Is there some truth to this? Absolutely! I defy you to show me a politician in Washington who doesn't have similar personality dynamics, if perhaps not quite to the degree of our former (and, one hopes, future) President. Those dynamics are virtually a prerequisite to seeking office at a high level; the shy, retiring, or introverted need not apply. And, unlike the vast majority of his detractors, Trump's self-confidence is justified by his history. He was a successful businessman. He was a successful television star. His first foray into politics was a success. Donald Trump built real things and created real value. He hasn't spent his life as a talking head spewing CO2 or a politician handing out other people's money. His ability to succeed in multiple fields speaks to a level of competence most can only envy. That envy is a primary source[1] of the most vitriolic rhetoric directed at the President, and if you look closely at just who's saying what when they attack it's easy to see.

That Trump makes no apologies for his self-confidence is one of his better features. His honesty in openly promoting himself and his policies is a refreshing, long-overdue change from the stale, fetid dissembling and half-hearted praising-with-faint-damns of other politicians. Donald J. Trump is one of the very few politicians that say what they mean and mean what they say, and that is why I personally have zero problems with any of the above-mentioned traits. Watching Trump's competence be a slap in the face to the "everybody gets a trophy" no-winner mindset of the equal-outcome Left is just a bonus.

What sets President Trump apart from the rest of the political herd is that he came to politics late in life and then refused to take on the "distinguished" trappings expected of politicians. You'll find precious few sweet-but-meaningless words, deferential behaviors towards opponents, and "respect for the institutions and traditions" so beloved by the denizens of the Imperial District of Corruption. Trump's lack of a filter when he speaks and tweets (now Truths) continues to be a gale-force blast of fresh air howling through the miasma of the Swamp. Considering that most ordinary people's "respect" for the Washington bureaucracy and Congress as a whole typically runs somewhere between toenail fungus and amoebic dysentery, Trump's demeanor isn't that much of a negative, especially with his supporters.

Watching the chattering, nattering nabobs and bouncing bobbleheads of the commenting class lose their (alleged) minds on a daily basis because of Donald J. Trump never gets old, and never will. They know this, they're helpless against it, and it's just one more reason they hate him and all those who support him.

I have avoided mentioning any other MAGA leaders, with the obvious exception being President Trump. I've done this out of fear that I could never hope to name even a few of the better ones. Since I don't wish to slight any, none gets a mention on these pages. Sorry, kids; just trying to be fair.

Deceased Senator John McCain gets special mention because he deserves it.[2] He was for years the prototypical "moderate Republican" (aka Republican In Name Only, or RINO), an Establishment shill, and the poster boy for the one big Uniparty and the corruption it feeds and is fed by within the DC Swamp. He is included as an example of how NOT to be a MAGA Patriot or a Constitutional conservative.

As a wise mentor told me decades ago: "No Mentor is completely worthless. Some may serve as bad examples." John McCain wasn't completely worthless. Of all the many, many politicians I love to loathe, he's several of them, all by himself. There may be another name or two scattered throughout this book, who may or may not be completely worthless. I leave such judgments up to the reader.

I've deliberately left out my political "Love to Loathe" list because this is a book, not a set of encyclopedias. Yes, it's that long.

In the Introduction to his recent book ***Beyond Biden***, former Speaker of the House Newt Gingrich had this to say:

> "After observing the first year of Joe Biden's presidency, I am convinced the 2020 election was a detour, and not a turning point."

With respect, Mr. Speaker, I disagree.

The Biden regime foisted on this nation by the stolen election of 2020 hasn't been a detour—it's been a derailment. Brandon's handlers have for all intents and purposes been working diligently to finish the "fundamental transformation" of America, started by his old boss Barry Soetoro, into a mere shadow of the great nation it once was.

I say "handlers" because, in all seriousness, Joe Biden has been little more than a prop to be led out, told to "just sign it", try to read the teleprompter without babbling too much, then not get lost or fall down as he exits, stage left. This was obvious from the day of his Inauguration when he was caught mumbling his stage directions to himself. It's sad, pathetic, and arguably the most public case of elder abuse in recent memory.

In deference to Speaker Gingrich, it took a bit more than a year for the full impact of Biden's (more accurately, his puppeteers and minders) policies to manifest. The summer of 2022's record-breaking gas prices, inflation rates, and ongoing supply chain issues took months to appear largely because of the residual positive inertia of the Trump economy. What began with killing the Keystone Pipeline on Biden's first day ultimately resulted in the Misery Index Summer of '22. The botched withdrawal from Afghanistan showed the world that America had returned to "leading from behind" with a vengeance. As I write this, we're pouring treasure (and nigh-irreplaceable missiles and other weapons, if China's Xi takes Taiwan and destroys TSMC's chip production lines) into a proxy war against Russia that we could well do without. The wheels are coming off the COVID narrative, order is collapsing in our great cities, and America is a laughing stock globally. More often than not, other leaders aren't taking Brandon's calls, and the ones that do generally ignore what the Dementoid in Chief has to say.

I won't even mention the collected wisdom and word salads of our Vice President, Kamalamadingdong Harris (with apologies to the Edsels[3]). Thankfully, that's already been done[4] so I don't have to bother with it.

Joe Biden has been a complete, total, and unmitigated disaster from the get-go, and now the country is in far worse shape than it was when Trump took office.

More and more people are realizing that the 2020 election was indeed rife with fraud and manipulation, to the point of having been stolen from President Trump. As Steven Bannon is fond of saying, "elections have consequences, stolen elections have catastrophic consequences." We are now seeing those catastrophic consequences firsthand.

Two-plus years of Progressive policies on energy, spending, climate and everything else being shoved down our collective throats have shown Americans just why Progressivism is toxic and unworkable. The "incredible transition" of a vibrant economy into a poor imitation of itself running on solar, wind, unicorn farts and pixie dust has demonstrated just how stupidly myopic the Green New Deal is in practice. Telling people who can't afford to fill up their tanks to just "buy an electric car" (with an average sticker price in excess of $66,000[5]) isn't a serious energy policy—it's a statement about just how far out of touch you are with the reality of everyday Americans.

The mood of the country is ugly and deteriorating by the day. The Left continues to fan the flames of partisan rhetoric, and the side drafts are feeding those on the Right, as well.

Best of all, the Democrat's Inflation Reduction (or Revved-Up) Act includes adding an additional 87,000 IRS agents who'll be hired to use deadly force on recalcitrant citizens. We remember Lois Lerner and Obama's IRS targeting the Tea Party and other conservative groups—how can this possibly end well?

Have the Regime's masterminds forgotten that America is 2-for-2 for bloody revolutions started over taxes and revenues? That little party in Boston harbor? Taxes. Mr. Lincoln's statement that, "if the South goes, where will we get our revenue?"[6] pretty much sums up old Abe's motivation for beginning the Late Unpleasantness.

Or, is it possible the Democrats haven't forgotten their history (real history[7], not that 1619 Project hogwash[8]), and this new army of Revenuers is more than just a convenient end-run around that pesky little posse comitatus thing?

This will NOT end well, at least in the short term.

What may happen is that enough froggies realize just how close to boiling they've come, and it's either jump out of the pot or be frog legs on the Liberal World Order menu (with a side of WEF bugs). There are signs that the fear of that jump into uncertainty is becoming less worrisome than the certain fate that awaits on the Progressive plate. These signs are why the Elites are anxious, why gun sales are spiking, and why more people are paying attention to politics and elections every day.

Virginia's 2021 election has given Patriots a model to follow for future elections—every single box has to be monitored from poll opening to final counting, tallying and reporting. 2000 Mules[9] ripped the scales from millions of eyes, exposing the fraud-o-rama that is drop box stuffing, and now other films like the [S]election Code[10] are piling on with more evidence of what really happened in 2020. Mike Lindell's herculean efforts[11] to expose systemic fraud at the level of the voting machines grind on, at tremendous personal cost to him. And finally, the MAGA Movement is poised to change into a bona fide political philosophy and force to be reckoned with inside the Republican Party and in elections all across the country.

This is not a recapitulation or review of the events of November 2020, nor is it a discussion of the successes and failures of Trump's four years in office. It is not intended to be a tactical manual for winning elections or addressing the Progressive agenda in our schools, communities, businesses, and State Houses.

This book is about how the forces that created the MAGA Movement in 2015 had been decades in the making. It's about how Donald J. Trump was the right man at the right moment with the right vision to take advantage of those forces and forge them into a successful campaign for the White House. It's about how the MAGA Movement is the polar opposite of the Progressive movement of the last 100+ years. Unlike every Progressive since Woodrow Wilson, MAGA seeks not to replace that pesky, inconvenient Constitution and the inefficient Republic it describes, but rather to restore them.

The Progressives are those self-congratulatory Elites and "fancy people who imagine themselves to be philosopher kings",[12] part of Codevilla's "Ruling Class"[13] who obviously know better than we bitter clingers, we basket of Deplorables, we semi-fascists, we threats to democracy.

Who are the people of the MAGA Movement? They are those People who believe in those unalienable rights endowed by their

Creator, and in a government established to secure those rights, justly empowered by the consent of the governed. They see what the Progressives have to offer, and do NOT consent to it, or to being ruled by them, in any way, shape, form or fashion.

They are the millions of Americans who want to put America First, Make America Great Again, and keep it that way!

And they are the People this book was written for.

ONE

The Origins Of The Maga Movement

"President Trump's election is a reaction against the Left's all-out assault on all that is good and true in America, an assault seen perhaps most clearly in the impact the Left's culture war has had on middle America—the patriotic, working-class Americans which the Left regards as both deplorable and dispensable."—Sebastian Gorka[1]

THE PHENOMENON OF DONALD J. Trump and the MAGA Movement didn't just spring into existence, it grew from a nation undergoing a "fundamental transformation" that many citizens did not want or need. MAGA's success was largely due to eight years of Obama, the 2008 financial crisis, and the Troubled Asset Relief Program (TARP). These events helped prepare the nation for a candidate like Trump, who spoke to ordinary men and women across the country. MAGA arose from the divide between the Ruling Class and the Country Class, which has been a long-standing issue in American politics. The Ruling Class, consisting of elites in academia, finance, and politics, has long seen themselves as superior to the Country

Class, who focus on real-world results, merit and traditional values. The Obama administration exacerbated this divide, preparing the way for the MAGA movement. Trump's campaign slogan, "Make America Great Again," became the rallying cry for the movement. Trump's plain-spoken, direct, and focused approach to campaigning was a breath of fresh air for a nation tired of empty words and political lies. Trump positioned himself as the anti-Obama, promising to put America First and restore the values of the Founders. By doing so, Donald J. Trump turned the Country Class into the MAGA Movement, and together they made history.

THE PHENOMENON of Donald John Trump and the Make America Great Again Movement may have begun with an escalator descent in June 2015, but it did not spring into existence *de novo*. The phenomenon and movement both sprouted and grew in the fertile soil of a nation undergoing a "fundamental transformation" into a form many of its citizens neither wanted nor felt it needed.

It's unlikely that Trump and the MAGA Movement would have been so successful had not the country endured eight years of the Obama administration, the 2008 financial crisis, and the Troubled Asset Relief Program (TARP).[2] Two terms of Obama after eight years of Bush II, eight years of Clinton & Clinton, and four years of Bush I prepared the nation for a brash, outspoken, egotistical billionaire real estate mogul turned reality TV star to be accepted as a Presidential candidate.

It's nothing short of remarkable that Donald J. Trump's Presidential announcement and subsequent campaign spoke so strongly to ordinary men and women across the country. That his campaign slogan, Make America Great Again, became the MAGA Movement—a movement that may well outlive its founder—is no less remarkable.

No great political movement appears out of nowhere. Political movements arise to fill a need, to satisfy a demand. That need or demand must have been created by something—a crisis, a failed leader, an external threat, or a sufficient build-up of societal pressure and discontent beyond that which the established parties and leaders can manage using customary measures. Typically, there is no single inciting factor that creates a political movement. Rather, a combination of stressors builds up until the old system's coping mechanisms fail.

There were a number of stressors on the American system in the latter years of the Obama administration, but it was decades of accumulated discontent with Washington's "business as usual" that created an opening for Trump to leverage as a Presidential candidate.

Obama and his appointees, and to a lesser extent the Clintons (because Bill and Hillary were, as they often said, a "two for one" special), had made it perfectly clear that they were better than the rest of us. Words like "bitter clingers" and phrases like "people just make bad choices" were the rule, not the exception during those long years. They were Elites, they surrounded themselves with other Elites, and they weren't the least bit reluctant to let non-elites know it. This attitude caused a bit of friction, but there was a sense of destiny in both the Clinton and Obama administrations that steamrollered most objections made by the heathens out in Flyover Country.

Naturally, this didn't go unnoticed.

In a 2010 American Spectator article "America's Ruling Class and the Perils of Revolution",[3] (later expanded into the book *The Ruling Class*, with a foreword by Rush Limbaugh), Professor Angelo M. Codevilla laid out the basic division of America into the

Ruling Class and the Country Class. Predating Trump's entry into the Presidential race, **The Ruling Class** describes the genesis of the Ruling Class of Elites and the essential differences between them and the Country Class. No other work (that I've found) does a better job of describing just how far apart the Ruling and Country Classes were in terms of their basic outlook, philosophy and goals.

While the two classes have been at odds for decades, the divide between them widened considerably with the TARP program, Obamacare, and the general policies and tone of the Obama administration. The Tea Party reflected this new level of animosity between the classes, but within a few years, the Tea Party faded into near-obscurity. Since 2015, the American political landscape has been dominated by the struggle between the Democratic Party, now largely controlled by Progressives and Socialists, and the MAGA Movement, personified in Donald J. Trump.

The Democrats and their Establishment Republican allies clearly were (and are) the Uniparty of the Ruling Class. Just as clearly, Trump and the MAGA Movement embody the Country Class. As an incarnation of the Country Class, the MAGA Movement is just the latest force to oppose a varied collection of Elitists, most of them identifying as Leftists, stretching back at least to the early part of the 20th Century.

As Professor Codevilla said in the Introduction to **The Ruling Class**:

> *"It is about the fact that America now divides ever more sharply into two classes, the smaller of which holds the commanding heights of government, from which it disposes in ever greater detail of America's economic energies, from which it ordains new ways of living as if it had the right to do so, and from which it*

asserts that that right is based on the majority class' stupidity, racism, and violent tendencies.

The other class' position is analogous to that of the frog that awoke to the fact that it was being slow-boiled only when getting out of the pan would require perhaps more strength and judgment than it had left."[4]

The divisions between the Ruling Class, always by far the numerical minority, and the majority Country Class developed over many years. The Ruling Class established themselves as Elites with a bi-coastal power base clustered around high-end academia, urban financial, social and technological centers and the nation's capital. Among themselves, they weren't self-proclaimed so much as self-assumed to have higher status. Since they were really the only people who mattered in the social and political circles that mattered (namely, theirs), it didn't have to be proclaimed—it was understood. Their superiority was, to them, as basic and inviolate as the law of gravity.

The Country Class, in comparison, were all the rest—the people who made real things, mined and farmed and manufactured, and went about their days without much thought about the power, influence and money games so beloved by the elites.

Describing America's Country Class is problematic because it is so heterogeneous. It has no privileged podiums, and it speaks with many voices, which are often inharmonious. It shares above all the desire to be rid of rulers it regards as inept and haughty. It defines itself practically in terms of reflexive reactions against the rulers' defining ideas and proclivities—e.g., ever-higher taxes and expanding government, subsidizing political favorites, social engineering, approval of abortion, etc.

—*The Ruling Class*, Ch. 4

Sweaty, dirty, and busy working for a living, the Country Class was generally dismissed by the Elites as being of little consequence in the Elite's world.

The Ruling Class was, and still is, the self-assured and self-proclaimed "best and brightest"—as they'll be more than happy to tell you. They attend the "best" schools, know all the "best" people and have a remarkable uniformity of thought about what's "best" in every sphere. As the government's size and power has grown, so has the ability of the Ruling Class to navigate the bureaucracy that has grown with it. While this began with Woodrow Wilson's progressive Presidency, it kicked off in earnest when Franklin Delano Roosevelt created the modern American bureaucratic state:

> *"Franklin Roosevelt began the process that turned the Chautauqua Class into rulers by bringing them into his administration. FDR described America's problems in technocratic terms. America's problems would be fixed by a "brain trust." Power would define who was brainy and who was not. His New Deal's solutions —the administrative state, made up of the alphabet-soup of "independent" agencies that have run America ever since—turned many progressives into powerful bureaucrats, and then into lobbyists."*

—*The Ruling Class*, Ch. 2

They came to Washington to do good, and did well, as the saying goes. Then, having no reason to leave, they stayed. In staying, they created, nurtured and expanded the bureaucratic state far beyond even FDR's wildest dreams. They began acquiring their own power to first interpret, then make and implement policy on their own, without any interference from Congress or Presidents. Federal worker's unions and generous regulations grew up to expand their power and made firing them virtually impossible. The bureaucracy developed its own rites and rituals, and any mere elected official quickly came to learn that one attacked them at one's peril.

As the people most directly responsible for doling out the largesse appropriated by Congress, the bureaucracy has long been the true holder of the purse strings. Congress may authorize and the President may sign budgets and continuing resolutions to keep the money flowing, but it is the bureaucracy that ensures the paperwork is done and the checks are cut.

They have the gold. They make the rules. Who really has the power?

The Ruling Class knows that the path to true power lies through the ability to navigate the bureaucracy. They speak bureaucratese fluently and navigate red tape and administrative minutiae as easily as fish swim in water. And, since growing government and bureaucratic power is a cornerstone of Leftist (collectivist) philosophy, the Ruling Class inevitably drifted further and further in that direction.

The Country Class, on the other hand, generally distrust government officials, agencies, and their associated flunkies and minions. They have little or no time for the bureaucracy and its pettifoggery because, quite frankly, they are busy trying to live their lives. "Government governs best that governs least", a concept that is anathema to the Ruling Class, is a basic tenet of the Country Class.

> *"The Country Class is not anti-government, just nongovernmental. It views the way people live their lives as the result of countless private choices rather than as the consequence of someone else's master plan."*

—*The Ruling Class*, Ch. 4

The Country Class tends to focus on actual results, not how well your report says you did when your project is allegedly finished. The Country Class is much more of a meritocracy, instead of the little-to-no-consequences-for-failure, relationship-driven social circles of the Elites and the bureaucrats.

> *"In general, the Country Class includes all those in stations high and low who are aghast at how relatively little honest work yields, by comparison with what just a little connection with the right bureaucracy can get you."*

—*The Ruling Class*, Ch. 4

Finally, the Country Class continues to cling to traditional values—home, family, God, limited government, the Constitution, self-reliance and responsibility—that are at best considered passé by the Ruling Class.

At worst, these traditional values have come to be maligned by the Leftist Elites of the Ruling Class as racist, fascist, patriarchal, homophobic, xenophobic, trans-phobic, regressive, anti-woman, denialist, etc., etc. *ad infinitum*. Since the labels shift so often, spending a few minutes seeing what's trending on Twitter or watching MSNBC is generally a good way to identify the offense of the moment.

An excellent analogy for the Left's constantly changing "evil *de jour*" can be found in Chapter 2 of Vox Day's **SJWs Always Lie**, where he compares Social Justice Warriors (SJWs, the Left's most vocal members) to a school of fish:

"It may be useful to think of SJWs as a school of hypersensitive fish, every single one of which is capable of rapid changes of direction based on the most minute signals from the fish on either side of them. This is why large numbers of SJWs can go from declaring black to be white to be blue to be red in rapid succession, all without ever appearing to notice that what they are all saying now is completely different than what they were all saying before. And woe to the SJW who fails to keep up and doesn't change his tune in time with the others!"

This, perhaps more than any other single feature, is what separates the Country Class from the shock troops of the Ruling Class Elites. The Elites are constantly alert for the next cause, the next injustice, the next outrage that must be addressed. Invariably, this will require new laws, new programs, new regulations and/or other expansions of government power. Once identified, their spox[5] and media mouthpieces sound the alarm (typically dropping yesterday's cause like a hot potato) to mobilize the foot soldiers. Cue trending hashtags, protests, poorly-made sign-waving, and copious outpourings of emotive Sturm und Drang demanding that it be made all better, right f*cking now!

The Country Class, in contrast, desires consistency and stability. They get up, go to work, raise their families, go to church, interact with their friends and neighbors and try to build better lives for themselves. They want to maintain the communities that are generally working for them. When changes need to be made, the preference of the Country Class is to make those changes directly and locally, without them being imposed by bureaucrats from on high. Members of the Country Class can't drop everything to chain-tweet or rush to the barricades—they have jobs, kids in school to pick up, and lives to lead. The Country Class isn't terribly fond of abrupt change or any "fundamental transformation", especially as a consequence of "mostly peaceful protests". As a group, the Country Class are "conservative" in the truest sense of the word.

In contrast, the only thing the Ruling Class Elites want to "conserve" is the system that keeps them in power.

The separation between the two classes became impossible to ignore between 2008 and 2010, which Codevilla traces to the 2008 TARP program, the lavish spending of the Obama administration and the Taxed Enough Already (TEA) Party Movement this federal largesse inspired.

> *"Although after the election of 2008, most Republican office holders argued against the Troubled Asset Relief Program, against the subsequent bailouts of the auto industry, against the several "stimulus" bills and further summary expansions of government power to benefit clients of government at the expense of ordinary citizens, the American people had every reason to believe that many Republican politicians were doing so simply by the logic of partisan opposition. After all, Republicans had been happy enough to approve of similar things under Republican administrations. Differences between Bushes, Clintons, and Obamas are of degree, not kind. Moreover, the 2009–10 establishment Republicans sought only to modify the government's agenda, while showing eagerness to join the Democrats in new grand schemes, if only they were allowed to."*
>
> --***The Ruling Class***, Introduction

As the Bush II Presidency wound down, the country was suddenly told that the financial system, specifically the nation's biggest banks, was about to collapse. Urgent action was needed to prevent the Apocalypse, and the Troubled Asset Relief Program (TARP) was unveiled.

Very little was actually explained to the average Joe and Jane American. The news reported that something on Wall Street had gone catastrophically wrong and would pull everything else down with it unless something drastic was done immediately. TARP was enacted, and most regular people felt they had little or no say in it. Suddenly, gazillions of tax dollars were poured into the banks, Wall Street, and firms that most people had only heard about in passing on the news. Then, those of us in Flyover Country were told that TARP was doing more, buying up other "assets", without any good explanation for that, either.

In the real world where the Country Class lives, a screw-up of that magnitude would have seen heads roll, if not criminal prosecutions and trials with lengthy sentences. As many of us recall, there was a glaring lack of this during 2008–2010 (or any time afterward). What the Country Class saw were Elites of the Ruling Class shrugging and going on about their business—business that had been saved with literal pallets of tax dollars. Work for a too-big-to-fail bank that just happens to be a generous source of campaign contributions? Never fear, TARP is here! Mess up so badly that the entire world could go into a depression? Oh well, these things happen; the US taxpayer will cover it. No worries.

And people wonder why the Taxed Enough Already Party sprang up.

The 2008 financial crisis and subsequent TARP also made it glaringly obvious that there was essentially no difference between the Blues and Reds in DC. George C. Wallace's statement[6] that there isn't "a dime's worth of difference" between Republicans and Democrats in Washington was never more true than when TARP was enacted. Alleged free-market Republicans couldn't seem to swallow the "too big to fail" argument fast enough, and when a few wags dared to ask if this didn't mean the failing banks weren't "too big to live" those wags—and their scandalous, heretical statements—were quickly shushed. Those who expected to see Sherman anti-trust cases or similar actions in the wake of TARP would be sorely disappointed.

And so, the Bush II years ended with a flapping TARP…and then along came Obama.

Barry Soetoro, aka Barack Hussein Obama, was elected President of the United States in 2008. In hindsight, his election seems inevitable, but in those halcyon days of 2007–2008, it was anything but. In truth, in 2006, had you asked the average citizen their opinion about then-Senator Obama, the typical response would have been "who?".

Early in 2007, the GOP contenders began vying for the nomination, with ultra-establishment Senator John McCain, the eventual nominee, being just one of the herd. While there was some excitement from non-establishment favorite Ron Paul, actor Fred Thompson, firebrand Alan Keyes, and Governor Mike Huckabee early on, the field quickly narrowed to favor McCain after the early primaries and initial debate. Despite Huckabee, Romney, and Ron Paul all receiving some votes at the 2008 Republican Convention, McCain won easily on the first ballot. By that time, most of the other contenders had given him their endorsements as they fell by the wayside. It was in most respects just another Republican nomination cycle, only exciting to the wonks and political junkies of the world. To most Americans, it was on par with watching paint dry on the excite-o-meter, especially as McCain became the clear front-runner.

The lackluster McCain did manage to generate some excitement when he nominated populist Sarah Palin as his running mate, but her popularity—vastly greater than McCain's—caused the campaign to throttle her back on a more or less regular basis. That the campaign eventually began having the pair tour together was a necessity to hide Palin's ability to fill venues easily, while McCain appeared to have trouble filling the back room at Denny's.

McCain's tenure in the Senate (he was first elected in 1987), questionable conservative record and sobriquet of "Songbird" McCain while a prisoner of war in Vietnam (1967-1973) for allegedly "singing like a bird" to his captors in exchange for preferential treatment[7] all contributed to McCain's low appeal to average Republicans and Independents in the general election.

On the Democratic side, in early 2007 it was assumed that Hillary Clinton would be the party's Presidential nominee. However, a very junior freshman Senator from Chicago dared to enter the race. Obama's team managed to go toe-to-toe with the Clinton machine and, surprisingly, took the nomination from Her. It was one of the most hard-fought party contests in recent memory, with a brokered convention being seriously considered[8] before Obama finally edged out the win.

In the 2008 general election, what had been predicted to be two establishment titans going at one another wound up being the inexperienced-but-inspirational "Magic Negro"[9] (as one writer for the Los Angeles Times dubbed Obama[10]) against Low-Energy McCain.

Surprising absolutely no one, Obama declined to name Hillary as his Vice Presidential nominee, opting instead for veteran Senator Joe Biden. Party stalwart Biden, most notable for his long history of 'foot in mouth' disease[11] and gaffes[12] was obviously chosen to reassure non-minority and establishment Democrats, as well as to be

Obama's life insurance policy. Given the Clinton Curse™—the trail of bodies who succumbed to fatal proximity to Bill & Hillary in tragic, sometimes mysterious ways—more than a few tongues wagged that VP Hillary would only have that particular job for a few weeks after Barry's inauguration before receiving a promotion. Obama did eventually name Hillary as his Secretary of State, which no doubt did wonders for his peace of mind and ability to sleep with both eyes closed over the next eight years.

That Hillary no doubt managed to alleviate her disappointment at not being #2 on the ticket by leveraging her position as Secretary of State into massive benefits for the Clinton Foundation has been covered elsewhere[13]. Her record at State and elsewhere would later come up during the 2016 Presidential campaign, and be one of many rallying cries for MAGA supporters—"Lock Her Up!"

Obama campaigned on "Hope and Change", while McCain...well, he probably had a campaign slogan, but nobody remembers it, so who cares? It certainly didn't help McCain's general popularity when he shut down his campaign to go back to Washington to help pass (i.e., ram through) the wildly unpopular TARP package (a January 2009 CNN poll showed 80% of voters opposed the package) and bail out the banks with taxpayer money. Meanwhile, Obama was filling stadiums with lofty rhetoric (so long as his teleprompter was working) and the promise of making history as the first "post-racial" President.

Despite serious questions—thoroughly downplayed if not ignored outright by the MSM—about his lack of record and experience, his sparse educational achievements, his sexuality, his drug use, his religion, his true parentage and even his eligibility for the office (a natural-born Kenyan cannot be President), many voters of all races and political leanings bought into the narrative of putting America's troubled past to rest by electing the nation's first Black President. After all, Obama was "the first mainstream African-American who is articulate and bright and clean and a nice-looking guy"[14] according to his then-primary opponent Biden[15].

That, and he wasn't RINOstablishment poster child John McCain.

After the election, the former Mr. Soetoro's "Hope and Change" abruptly switched to "Elections have consequences. I won." As Victor Davis Hanson so aptly put it in the opening section of ***The Case for Trump***:

> *"Obama began governing the United States as if there really were two Americas, with more an attitude of triumphalist "I won" than his earlier inclusive "hope and change."*
>
> *"That partisanship was not unusual for a president, but one-sidedness perhaps was for someone variously described ecumenically by media stalwarts as a "god," or who, in his own words, would begin to lower the seas and cool the overheated planet."*
>
> *--**The Case for Trump**, Introduction*

Initially, it worked for him. Obama had control of the White House and Congress. He was awarded the Nobel Peace Prize in 2009 for his "extraordinary efforts to strengthen international diplomacy and cooperation between peoples" and for fostering a "new climate" in international relationships. In other words, he got the Big Prize not for anything he'd actually done, but just for what he'd said. Or perhaps, Ehrenstein was right when he called it 'Magic': "It's the way he's said it that counts the most."[16]

In subsequent years, some members of the Nobel Committee spoke about that particular award—arguably the world's largest Participation Trophy EVER—and their regret over the decision.[17] Better late than never, I suppose.

Early in his first term, Obama spent most of his political capital and goodwill on the effort to pass the Affordable Care Act (ACA), which was rapidly labeled "Obamacare". The massive federalization of America's healthcare sector had long been a Democratic dream. Many remembered how during Bill Clinton's tenure in the Oval Office, First Spouse Hillary had led a group that eventually drew up "Hillarycare". That particular abomination never passed Congress, but its core concepts formed the basic structure upon which the ACA was built. Eventually "deemed" to have passed the Senate by Democrat Speaker Nancy Pelosi[18] so that the bill could then be passed by the House[19] with no Republican support at all, the ACA became an albatross around the neck of Democrats at virtually every level of government.

Obama ran as an unfrightening moderate both in 2008 and 2012 (when he shellacked that RINO's RINO, the whitest white man on Earth, "Mittens" Romney) but he governed from the far Left. His dismal record both at home and abroad, his inept handling of the economy, and a near-constant stream of scandals[20] including (but certainly not limited to) weaponizing the IRS against conservative groups and the Fast & Furious gun-running debacle are well-documented and remembered. Obama's "lead from behind" strategy greatly diminished America's standing globally, and his efforts to "fundamentally transform" our society gave us the Asinine Care Act, Common Core, the auto industry bailouts, miserable economic performance and an increase in racial tension to levels not seen since the 1960s.

The gap between Obama's promised Hope and Change and what he actually delivered over eight years was staggering. What he did do, however, was thoroughly wreck his party at both the state and federal levels:

> *"As a result of Obama's agendas, when the two-term president left office with final majority approval, his political legacy nevertheless was a blue atoll in an ocean of red. Over his tenure, his party had lost the House. It gave up the Senate. The majority of state legislature chambers (99-69) and governorships (33-17) were by 2017 Republican. Obama had given the Republicans a good chance at winning the Electoral College in 2016, and after the elections, not since 1920 had the Republican Party emerged stronger."*
>
> **—*The Case for Trump*, Ch. 1**

It was also a done deal that Hillary Clinton, having sold access to the State Department on the open market for eight years[21], would be Obama's successor. A crowded field of Republicans, and a few helpless, luckless, clueless Democrats began assembling to challenge Her in 2015. Still, the chattering arm of the Ruling Class was confident that no Republican could ever stand in the way of our first Woman President.

Then, something amazing happened.

Donald J. Trump rode down an escalator and said he was going to become our next President.

And he did.

> *"Trump challenged more than the agendas and assumptions of the political establishment. His method of campaigning and governing, indeed his very manner of speech and appearance, was an affront to the Washington political classes and media—and to the*

> norms of political discourse and behavior. His supporters saw the hysterical outrage that Trump instilled instead as a catharsis."
>
> --***The Case for Trump***, Introduction

Barack Obama did more than leave his party in ruins.[22] He hammered the healthcare system. He bailed out his buddies in the UAW, and let the banking bailouts roll unhindered. He let Hillary take the heat for bungling Benghazi. He loosed Lois Lerner and the IRS on conservative groups, especially the Tea Party, and left his AG Eric Holder holding the bag for the Fast and Furious fustercluck. He led from behind, drew meaningless lines in faraway sands and made America a laughing stock in the Club of Nations. His insipid economy inspired him to invoke a "magic wand" he didn't have that would be needed to restore American jobs long moved off-shore. He encouraged intersectionality, rewarded radicals and (anti-white) racists, and incited and inflamed passions against the evilest creatures to ever walk the face of the earth—heterosexual white males.

When the true history of the Obama Presidency is written decades from now, one fact will stand out above all the rest: Barack Hussein Obama made Donald J. Trump's Presidency possible.

For eight interminable years, Obama and his minions gave the country a taste of progressive utopia, and the Country Class did not care for it in the slightest. This was the fertile soil in which the MAGA movement grew so quickly and so well.

In 2013, Lawrence Sellen described his vision of what America post-Obama's "fundamental transformation" would look like:[23]

> *"Like "Nineteen Eighty-Four," Obama's dystopia will be a world of perpetual crisis, omnipresent government surveillance, misin-*

formation and manipulation by state-controlled media; all governed by a privileged, hedonistic and shallow political elite led by a quasi-divine party leader who enjoys an intense cult of personality and considers free will as a source of unhappiness."

—**Restoring the Republic—Arguments for a Second American Revolution**, Ch. 5

But, in all fairness, the Obamoids can't be solely credited with preparing the way for MAGA and Trump. The slow erosion of the limited federal government enshrined in the Constitution coupled with the rise of the bureaucratic state, had been decades, if not centuries, in the making.

The conflict between the Federalists, who desired a powerful central government, and the Anti-Federalists, who wanted more control at the level of the sovereign States, is as old as the nation itself. Patrick Henry[24] and the other Anti-Federalists were concerned about the possible power abuses of a strong central government. Given our current status, they were obviously correct in their concerns.

This Federalist-Anti-Federalist conflict reached a peaked from 1861—1865, with the Union victory ensuring the power and prestige of the federal government over the no-longer sovereign states. If that weren't bad enough, Teddy Roosevelt's split from the Republican Party and his third party (Progressive, or Bull Moose) run for the Presidency in 1912 divided the Republican vote and gave the election to Democrat Woodrow Wilson.

Wilson, an academician turned politician, was a great believer in the power of the government, especially the Elites within it, to know better than the average voter how things should be done. In Constitutional Government in the United States (1908), Wilson stated:

> *"The constitutional structure of the government has hampered and limited his (the President's) action in these significant roles, but it has not prevented it. . . . It is merely the proof that our government is a living, organic thing, and must, like every other government, work out the close synthesis of active parts which can exist only when leadership is lodged in some one man or group of men. . ."*[25]

To Wilson, the Constitution unnecessarily restrained the President, acting as the leader of a victorious Party, from fixing the problems faced by the nation. Like subsequent Progressives, he firmly believed in the ability, indeed the duty, of the Elites to guide the country down the proper path. Of course, that proper path would be the one chosen by the Elites themselves, without input or interference from those lesser beings, everyday Americans. Wilson's ideas were the genesis of the modern government-by-administrative-bureaucratic-elitist Ruling Class in America.

And so, the rise of the Ruling Class proceeded apace, through FDR, then the Great Society and the War on Poverty, the War on Drugs, the EPA, the Department of Education, Bush I, the Clintons, Bush II, the Department of Homeland Security, the Patriot Act, and then Obama. The reach and scope of government grew. Bureaucracies grew. Spending and deficits grew. The power of the Imperial Capitol in DC grew, and grew, and grew until we reached peak Wilsonianism in 2014, when President Obama said "I've got a pen and I've got a phone".[26] The Progressive dream seemed close to being realized during the Obama years. But to many, it was a nightmare.

This was America when Donald Trump launched his candidacy on that fateful day in June, 2015. An anemic economy, racial tension, and significant friction between the people (especially conservatives) and their government, after literally decades of the same old-same old policies from Washington regardless of who or what party was in charge. The Country Class had had enough of the Ruling Class' policies, sermonizing, hubris and lack of results.

As one conservative complained, "it doesn't matter who we elect, they all turn into John McCain."

That was NOT a compliment.

Defying all expectations, analysis, and reasoning of the Ruling Class, the Country Class found their champion in a brash, boisterous Orange Man with unbelievable hair.

Accurately sensing the country's mood, Trump immediately positioned himself as the anti-Obama. Instead of a fundamental transformation of America, he promised to put America First. Instead of repudiating America for its past sins, he celebrated it for its accomplishments. Make America Great Again as a slogan wasn't original to Trump—Ronald Reagan, among others, had used some form of it—but Trump made it his own. The Movement that formed around his campaign represented a restoration of the values of the Founders to MAGA Patriots. That promise—to restore America's Greatness—more than anything else, is why the billionaire reality TV star was able to speak so powerfully to so many average, ordinary people.

Trump spoke to the issues those people cared about. He offered real-world, concrete solutions to the problems tied to those issues. After decades of polished political platitudes and puerile policy pronouncements, Donald Trump was plain-spoken, direct and focused—a blast of fresh air for a nation tired of empty words and political lies. It was apparent from his first campaign speech in June 2015 that Donald J. Trump would NEVER turn into John McCain.

He would never be Mitt Romney. That, as much as anything, was what millions of MAGA patriots responded to so strongly.

Donald J. Trump turned the Country Class into the MAGA Movement. Together, they made history.

God willing, they will continue to make history as they Make America Great Again—Again!

TWO

But Is It Maga?

"This used to be a government of checks and balances. Now it's all checks and no balances."—Gracie Allen

FROM ITS INCEPTION, *Trump's candidacy was mocked as a joke, even as millions of supporters rallied under Trump's banner. His success was due to his ability to connect with average, everyday Americans who had been abandoned and ignored by the nation's Ruling Class. Red MAGA hats came to represent the hopes, dreams, fears, and aspirations of Patriots who had been ridiculed and dismissed by the political and pundit classes. For MAGA to avoid the fate of the Tea Party and continue to win elections, the MAGA movement must establish a set of basic principles to guide its growth and ease the way past those awkward moments when someone asks, "But is it MAGA?" Four basic questions can be used to determine if an idea is consistent with America First/MAGA ideals: promoting, protecting, defending, and advancing the cause of ordinary Americans, doing the same for America as a sovereign nation, being consistent with the ideals of the Founders, and being moral, just, and right.*

The MAGA Movement must inevitably grow beyond any single man, and these four questions will serve as touchstones against which new ideas, innovations, and policies can be judged as to their place within an America First/MAGA framework.

On June 16th, 2015, Donald J. Trump rode down the escalator into the lobby of the Tower that bears his name and announced his candidacy for President of the United States.

His speech was mocked and derided, and his campaign was considered a joke by the political and pundit classes, but his main themes—immigration, trade, war—and what would be his campaign's slogan—"Make America Great Again"—spoke to millions of men and women across the country.

Here was a billionaire real estate developer turned reality TV star, a man who turned his name into a brand and that brand into a global icon. And yet, he spoke to average, everyday Americans, especially those "bitter clingers" to their God and their guns, and they listened.

As the 2016 campaign went on, those men and women did more than listen. They flocked to rallies. They bought flags and bumper stickers and t-shirts. They started wearing bright red hats that said "Make America Great Again" in bold white letters.

They watched as Donald J. Trump stood against more than a dozen experienced politicians in the Republican debates, and did more than just hold his own. As the primary season ground on, those men and women flocked to the polls to support him. Somewhere between that day in June and Jeb! effectively falling out of the race (and forever tarnishing the exclamation point along the way), MAGA became the "official" abbreviation for Trump's slogan.

By the 2016 Republican National Convention, MAGA had solidified into a bona fide political movement with millions of people of all ages rallying together under Trump's banner. Those red MAGA hats had become an iconic symbol of Trump's campaign brand, and much more. The MAGA hat represented (and still represents) the hopes, dreams, fears, and aspirations of Patriots who had been abandoned and ignored by the Ruling Class of this nation for far too long.

As MAGA grew and those red hats spread, the laughter from the political and pundit classes took on a hysteric quality that would only escalate over time.

During the general election, MAGA Patriots were labeled "deplorables", ridiculed, dismissed, and scorned. The Democrats and their allies in the media, along with the Never-Trump RINOs, told them repeatedly just how awful Trump was, and how awful they were for supporting him. They didn't care. The more he and they were attacked, the more Trump's support grew, and the more red hats were sold.

Trump's Twitter bombs made the Left lose their (alleged) minds on a regular basis, and the Left never seemed to wise up to the fact that he frequently did that just to provoke them. The more he trolled them on social media, the more extreme their reactions became—and the MAGA movement loved it.

On election night 2016, MAGA Patriots waited, then cheered as Trump was declared the winner. Then came the triggering of the snowflakes, primal screams of shock and disbelief from those who were with Her, booming demand for safe spaces with coloring books and crayons for infantile adults, #TheResistance and Russia-RussiaRussia.

For four years, the MAGA Movement watched as President Trump was besieged from within and without, yet still managed to fulfill a shockingly high number of campaign promises. He worked diligently to build the Wall, led us to the greatest energy renaissance in our history,[1] and gave us a tremendous economy.[2]

And then COVID and the 2020 election happened.

Now, President Trump and his America First policies are sorely missed by those average, everyday Americans. Inflation at home and instability abroad are just two of the many disasters created by the Biden Regime. A politically-weaponized DoJ and FBI are targeting his associates and supporters, and the new "lethal force" IRS is about to be unleashed on MAGA supporters. Wokeness is the order of the day, and objecting to its age-inappropriate tenants being forced on one's children gets parents labeled "domestic terrorists".

The Mar-A-Lago raid, just like two impeachments, the January 6th investigation and too many lawsuits to count, are all part of the ongoing campaign to prevent Trump from being elected President again in 2024. Hopefully, these efforts will be unsuccessful, if for no other reason than to discourage similar egregious attacks in the future. Regardless, MAGA patriots need to recognize that President Donald J. Trump will not be with us forever. Either due to the machinations of the enemies of MAGA—myriad, vast, and powerful as they may be—or purely through time and biology, President Trump will need strong successors if the MAGA Movement is to persist, thrive, and continue to fight for our country.

For now, the MAGA Movement and its policies are those of Donald J. Trump. However, if the MAGA Movement is to avoid the fate of the Tea Party—having a few victories but ultimately being marginalized, corrupted, subsumed, and finally reduced to a shadow of its former self—then it will need a set of basic principles to serve as touchstones of just what truly is "MAGA".

Jim Hanson addressed this issue recently in American Greatness:[3]

> *"The problem is that Trumpism and Make America Great Again, by themselves, are not a coherent ideology, governing philosophy, or a political platform. And they are far too dependent on one man. We need to coalesce around something larger and more lasting. We need a movement that recognizes the dire situation of the country; and, has substantive solutions and the will to impose them on an unwilling bureaucracy. This must include the ability to explain these principles to a large enough number of American voters to win elections."*

The basis for such an ideology and governing philosophy is already present in the MAGA Movement, in the policies and statements of President Trump and others who espouse an America First agenda. It continues to grow and change, as is only natural for the guiding philosophy of a movement in its early years. Such growth is often uncomfortable and awkward, but the discomfort and awkwardness are not only necessary but ultimately beneficial—if used constructively to improve the final outcome. Like everything else in life, mistakes can serve as learning opportunities about what NOT to do next time.

The MAGA Movement is at the point where a set of basic principles must be established to guide this growth and help ease the way past those awkward moments when someone asks the question, "But is it MAGA?"

"Is it MAGA?" This question will inevitably arise as more and more people join the Movement. The ability to answer that question as to whether something is MAGA (or not) is essential to solidifying the MAGA brand as a viable political entity, not just a cult of personality. It is essential to creating a unified philosophy and ideology, from which positions and solutions logically flow. It is essential to telling average, everyday Americans what the MAGA Movement is and what it stands for, in plain terms they can easily understand.

Being able to answer "is it MAGA, or not?" is essential to the success of the Movement in the years and generations to come. Every successful movement must be able to point to the ideas they embrace. They must also be able to say, with reasonable certainty, what ideas they do NOT embrace. In fact, being able to confidently say something is NOT a MAGA idea is likely more important than being able to say it IS compatible with a pro-MAGA, pro-America First ideology. One only has to look at the Democratic Party to see how the introduction of new ideas that are inconsistent with long-held positions can drastically shift a movement's focus. Ronald Reagan[4] may have said it first—"I didn't leave the Democratic Party, the Democratic Party left me"—but he certainly hasn't been the only one.[5,6,7]

What's needed are a few simple criteria to judge if an idea is compatible with MAGA ideals, based on the merits of what is being questioned. These criteria can then guide the continued growth of a coherent ideological structure built on the foundation of President Trump's America First agenda. These criteria must also, of necessity and for the sake of the Movement, be separate from Trump the man.

Donald J. Trump started the MAGA Movement, and he will always be remembered and revered (in some circles, reviled) for it. Now, the MAGA Movement has grown beyond any single man, no matter how talented or capable that man may be. MAGA Patriots can be thankful that President Trump continues to lead, guide, and direct the Movement he began as it grows. As a parent, President Trump understands that children inevitably grow up to become their own people. The MAGA Movement is no different. Children become adults and go their own way, guided by what they have learned from their parents. The MAGA Movement must inevitably do the same.

I believe that four basic questions can be used to determine if an idea is consistent with America First/MAGA ideals. Properly used, these questions can serve as touchstones against which new ideas, innovations, and policies can be judged as to their place within an America First/MAGA framework, or not.

These four touchstone questions are not, in and of themselves, policy positions or platform planks. Rather, they reflect my understanding of principles that underlie the statements of President Donald J. Trump and those who truly support his desire to Make America Great Again.

If the answer to any of these questions is NO, then whatever is being questioned is clearly NOT MAGA. If the answer to all of them is YES, then the item in question MAY be MAGA—but this is not an absolute certainty, as you'll see below.

WHENEVER A POLICY, **law, regulation or other matter of the public interest is being considered, ask the following:**

- **Does it promote, protect, defend and/or advance the cause of ordinary Americans?**

- **Does it promote, protect, defend and/or advance the cause of America as a sovereign nation?**
- **Is it consistent with the ideals of the Founders, especially those expressed in the Declaration and the Constitution?**
- **Is it moral, just, and right?**

When answering these questions consider not only the purported benefits but also the costs, consequences, and effects, both intended and otherwise.

THESE FOUR QUESTIONS require honest judgments, made by honest MAGA Patriots, for their answers to have any real value. Sadly, the opponents of MAGA are well-versed in twisting their statements, reasons, rationalizations and arguments to further their anti-American, anti-MAGA goals. And, lest we forget, those who would thwart the MAGA agenda have a tendency to just flat-out lie to get what they want.

Whatever the policy being considered, these four questions provide a framework for assessing the "MAGA-ness" (or lack thereof) of a proposal. By having this framework available, it should be easier for future MAGA leaders to assess their ideas and stimulate discussion about exactly what these policies will do in the "real world". For too long, the Ruling Class and the Administrative-Bureaucratic State (ABS) have enacted and enforced policies, rules and regulations with little or no regard for their actual costs, benefits, or effects.

President Trump made some inroads into correcting the reality disconnect of the ABS in his first term, and we can only look forward in his second term to more efforts like his Schedule F Executive Order used to benefit the People, not the Ruling Class.

At some point, the MAGA torch will pass. We fervently hope and pray that it is not soon, but it will happen. At present, there are several strong contenders to become the next leaders of the MAGA Movement, and more will almost certainly arise. These leaders will not be President Trump, and they will have their own ideas and vision for MAGA. Also, as the national and global situation changes, new strategies will be needed to support the Constitutional Republic envisioned by the Founders.

Hopefully, these four questions will serve the MAGA Movement, its leaders, and its Patriot members well. With the continued blessings of Divine Providence, they will allow MAGA and its America First philosophy to endure for generations yet to come.

THREE

Maga, The Tea Party, And The Gop

"Experience hath shewn, that even under the best forms, those entrusted with power have, in time and by slow operations, perverted it into tyranny," —**Thomas Jefferson**

THE MAGA MOVEMENT *stands at a critical juncture. If MAGA is to survive, it must successfully become a bona fide wing of the GOP. The Tea Party, which preceded MAGA, ultimately faded away because it lacked a unifying voice during its critical period. The MAGA Movement's success thus far is due to having a single, widely acknowledged leader to carry the flag for the grassroots activists. Ideally, the MAGA Movement will take over the Republican Party and reshape it in accordance with the goals and ideals of the America First agenda. The MAGA Movement must not allow the RINO Establishment to hold the power within the Republican Party and must take action now if the Republic is to be saved. Electing MAGA candidates is critical to implementing the America First agenda and saving the country. It will take several cycles and will be an ongoing process for years to come as new wanna-be*

RINOs pop up, but the MAGA Movement will restore first the Republican Party and then this great Republic, the United States of America.

THE MAGA MOVEMENT stands at a critical juncture, not only for the nation but for the Movement itself. What began as a group of people supporting one man's political aspirations is now developing into a cohesive force within the Republican Party.

All political movements face critical moments from time to time. The MAGA Movement is hardly unique in this. Some succeed, like Republicans in the mid-1800s. Some do not, like the Whigs.

The ones we remember either failed in their critical moment and died; or overcame their particular crisis and became something... more. More resilient, more organized, more impactful, and more likely to survive and thrive for years to come.

If the MAGA Movement cannot successfully complete this transition and become a *bona fide* wing of the GOP, it risks falling to the same fate as the Tea Party that came before it.

The Tea Party began much as MAGA did, with one major difference. From the beginning, MAGA has had a single, widely acknowledged leader to carry the flag for the grassroots activists. The Tea Party had no such person.

Despite having highly motivated people, exceptional goals, and early successes, the Tea Party ultimately faded away because it lacked a unifying voice during this critical period. Without that strong voice, the Tea party never really coalesced into a national group. It stayed divided, with literally hundreds upon hundreds of grassroots organizations, each with its own leaders and specific goals. This division left the field wide open for any number of hucksters, scam artists, and snake oil salesmen who acted to the detriment, rather than the benefit, of the Tea Party, its members, and its candidates.[1]

Without a central figure, the Tea Party could never put forth a single, clear vision. There was never an inner circle to support that one leader and share the burden of creating the movement from the ground up. These inner circle members would have been the ones to flesh out overall policy goals, put forth consistent positions and (later) legislative packages, and in general create the organizational structure to carry the Tea Party forward.

This is not to say that many Tea Party groups didn't do excellent work—far from it. Their example continues to inspire many local MAGA and America First groups. Often, this is because Tea Party members continue to work to advance conservative goals as members of these other groups. The labels may have changed, but the people and their aims have not. Like the Free Soilers who merged with the newly-formed Republican Party in 1854, many individual Tea Partiers easily moved into the MAGA Movement.

Despite many people insisting that the Tea Party should take over the Republican Party[2] and remake it in its own image, this never happened. Instead, Tea Party legislators were elected, then "got to Washington and properly sank into the Swamp". They turned into Swamp Critters, or John McCains (same thing). Without a single person or small group speaking up for "the real Tea Party", it was all too easy for Establishment RINOs to co-opt some Tea Party language and positions publicly, while actively working to "crush"[3] those unwashed insurgents who dared to challenge the Establishment's power. This only increased the disillusionment of many rank-and-file Tea Party members.

By the 2016 election, the Tea Party had all but vanished. In 2018, it was officially pronounced dead.[4] Agree with those reports of its demise or not, there was a silver lining to the sad tale of the Tea Party's decline.

Donald J. Trump was able to build his successful presidential campaign, and the MAGA Movement, by drawing in many former Tea Party members early on. This would continue throughout the 2015-2016 primary season. In 2015, Tea Partiers were as frustrated as they had ever been, and still desperately looking for a way to restore the America they had been taught to revere all their lives. While some objected to deemphasizing fiscal conservatism, many Tea Partiers embraced Trump's populist nationalism—especially since RINOs like Mitch McConnell had repeatedly driven home the object lesson that talking about fiscal sanity inside the Beltway would be punished.

When Trump's candidacy offered them hope—perhaps their last hope, given what a President Hillary portended—and an option that was radically different from the other Republican candidates in 2015 and 2016? Tea Partiers took off their tricorn hats and traded them in for bright red MAGA caps in droves.

One movement splintered and faded away, but parts of its spirit were reborn into a new Movement. It is this new Movement, MAGA, that now must succeed where the Tea Party failed.

It has been glaringly obvious since the day candidate Trump announced his bid for the Presidency that the Republican Party and its controllers were not his friends. The Establishment RINOs and Never-Trumper's resistance to his campaign, both passive and active, and his subsequent Presidency is well-documented. Some of the most heinous of these persons actively supported the Democrats' efforts to impeach him, not once but twice! Fortunately, these particular RINOs seem to be rapidly disappearing from public view.[5]

Granted, there are a couple of exceptions to this who shall NOT be named here. They just won't go away, like an itchy rash in an embarrassing place. Hopefully, a strong MAGA poultice will prove efficacious for these lesions on the body politic in the very near future.

A majority of the GOP Establishment has been as staunchly against an accurate count of the legal votes in the 2020 election as any "No Evidence" shill on the Left. The worst of them have actively opposed most, if not all, of President Trump's actions subsequent to leaving office, including his ongoing 2024 campaign. Given this long-standing pattern of behavior, it's doubtful that these Never-Trump fools will ever change.

This being the case, it is imperative that the MAGA Movement take over the Republican Party and reshape it in accordance with the goals and ideals of the America First agenda.

MAGA Patriots have only two realistic alternatives to assuming control of the Republican Party. The first is to continue to work within the existing GOP as the Tea Party tried to do, knowing that a similar (bad) outcome is virtually guaranteed. The second option is to take the MAGA Movement—roughly two-thirds of the GOP, along with a significant number of disaffected Democrats and patriotic Independents—and form a new Party.

Most MAGA Patriots are not willing to tolerate allowing the RINO Establishment—who David Azzerad so perfectly described as "losers, cowards and grifters"[6]—to continue on as the "Democrat-Lite" section of the Ruling Class. They have no desire to be subjected to the same fate as the Tea Party. If MAGA Patriots had wanted more Republican slow-walk socialism and Dem-Lite behavior, they'd have voted for Jeb! (and shared the shame he brought to the poor exclamation point).

Been there. Done that. Got the shirt—burned it.

Many hoped that in the weeks and months after the 2020 election, President Trump would indeed leave the GOP altogether. When GOP operatives said, rightly, that if Trump left "the Republicans will never win another election!", more than a few MAGA Patriots laughed and said "Good!"

After all, it's not like the GOP Establishment has done much of anything for the Country Class in the last two or three decades, is it? Some of us are still waiting for that balanced budget, or term limits, or even for Republicans to act like they're, you know, REPUBLICANS. And where's that Repeal and Replace of Obamacare we were promised?

As one person quipped, "It's not like they did anything after they got elected except roll over for the Democrats, was it?"

Tucker Carlson summed up the feelings of many Americans in 2015-2016 quite nicely:

> *Trump's election wasn't about Trump. It was a throbbing middle finger in the face of America's ruling class. It was a gesture of contempt, a howl of rage, the end result of decades of selfish and unwise decisions made by selfish and unwise leaders. Happy countries don't elect Donald Trump president. Desperate ones do.*
>
> —***Ship of Fools****, Introduction*

The actions of the Republican Establishment since 2016 haven't done much of anything to salve that contempt or lessen that rage.

Those middle fingers are still itching to wave in the RINO's smug, self-satisfied faces.

Admittedly, the challenges involved in breaking the two-party death grip on our elections would make forming a new Party extremely difficult. When President Trump refused to do this in the aftermath of the November 2020 election, the window of opportunity for an effective schism and reformation into a new Party closed, at least for the time being. However, always in motion is the future.[7]

The nuclear option is always on the table whenever an American President walks into any negotiation, as a matter of long-standing policy. The RINO Establishment would do well to remember that leaving the GOP continues to be an option for the MAGA Movement.

You have been warned.

The RINO Establishment, despite being fewer in number than either the Tea Party or MAGA Movement, has continued to hold much of the power within the Republican Party. The Tea Party failed to take the reins of the GOP, which is the primary reason the Tea Party was so easily sidelined, subsumed, and squelched.

The MAGA Movement can not, and must not allow this to happen to itself and the America First agenda. The country has already gone too far down the road to Death by Progressivism. Action must be taken now if the Republic is to be saved. Fortunately, it seems this process is already underway, and good progress is being made in a number of areas.

MAGA candidates promoting an America First agenda eagerly sought out President Trump's endorsement in the 2022 cycle. The vast majority of those who gained his endorsement won their primaries, which speaks volumes to the ongoing power of Trump's appeal to Republican voters. These MAGA candidates did well in November's general election[8]--despite RINO sabotage[9] and another round of Democratic/Progressive election fraud as we saw in 2020.

If enough honesty can be forced upon the election system in 2024 to allow accurate counting of legal votes, then MAGA candidates WILL win. Electing MAGA candidates is critical to implementing the America First agenda and saving the country. Electing America First pro-MAGA candidates is also necessary to begin taking over the Republican Party, as elected MAGA officials can begin replacing RINOs up and down local and state party rosters. These local and state MAGA leaders will then be able to take the reins of the National Republican Party, changing its platform into an America First, MAGA-centric platform, and offering those who don't agree the choice to either a) convert or b) leave. Buh bye!

MAGA Patriots know firsthand what it is to be excluded from the Cool RINOs Club.[10] It's time the RINOs found themselves shut out of the party!

This will not happen overnight, nor in a single election cycle. It will take several cycles, and will be an ongoing process for years to come as new wanna-be RINOs pop up. There will always be those who will want to be more "accommodating" with the Progressives, for various reasons. These people will be well-funded (from guess where?) and come prepared for battle, spouting lofty phrases and lovely-sounding goals—but we know from experience just where that leads.

"Accommodating" and "compromising" with the Left got us into this predicament to begin with. Why should we repeat those mistakes? Thank you, no.

We are engaged in a continual struggle for not just the hearts and minds, but the very soul of our nation. Our opponents have worked diligently for decades to bring us to this point. It would be unreasonable to expect it to take anything less than decades to reverse the damage that has been done. The restoration of the Constitutional Republic envisioned by the Founders will be a long-term project. It is one that we should already be teaching our children and our grandchildren to carry on long after we are gone.

We preserve the Republic every time we tell the stories of the Founders and teach the younger generations about the Declaration and its meaning. We must continue to teach our real history. We must explain the ideas and ideals embedded in the Constitution, and why they matter. We must never forget the brave men and women who brought this nation into being, and why we must always work to preserve it.

With the example of the Founders in mind, and by the grace of God, the MAGA Movement will restore first the Republican Party, and then this great Republic, the United States of America.

FOUR

Maga Enemies

"The world is governed by very different personages from what is imagined by those who are not behind the scenes."—Benjamin Disraeli

MAGA HAS BECOME a powerful political movement despite disrespect, dismissal, and vicious attacks from its enemies. In the 2020 election, the Left and their allies had no qualms about using any means necessary "to protect the election" and "ensuring it would be free and fair, credible and uncorrupted". In other words, the wrong person, Donald J. Trump, was not declared the winner, regardless of the number of legal votes cast for him. It's not only foreign nations like China that would prefer a weak American leader over a strong one like Trump, but also America's "Enemies Domestic"—Ruling Class Elites, their allies, apparatchiks, and useful idiots. These groups have weaponized the U.S. Government to attack Trump and his supporters, and until significant changes are made MAGA can only support those leaders who are targeted by the Regime. Among MAGA's domestic enemies are the

Screeching Socialists, Status Quo Deep Staters, Neo-Clowns, Globalist Ghouls, Tech Lords and the Uniparty Establishment. The MAGA movement and its supporters face ongoing attacks from these Enemies Domestic who want to tear down the Constitution and the Republic it describes—a government of, by, and for the People. To defeat them, MAGA Patriots must be aware of the Left's tactics, and be willing to engage them at every turn. MAGA must be unafraid to use every legal resource available, and understand that restoring the Republic will not be any single act, but a process.

MAGA began as a campaign slogan for an unlikely political candidate. It became a Movement that swept that man into office—the first President in our nation's history with a background in business and entertainment, without any military or political experience. Along the way, that man and his supporters were dismissed, disrespected, demeaned, downplayed, degraded, and viciously attacked with intent to destroy. Nonetheless, that Movement re-elected their President a second time, only to have the election stolen from them.

The MAGA Movement must be heavily involved in securing the integrity of our elections, for obvious reasons. The lesson of 2020 is that the Left and their allies have no compunction against using any means necessary to secure their electoral aims.

In February 2021, Mary Ball wrote in Time magazine[1] about the coordinated efforts against President Trump in the 2020 election:

> "There was a conspiracy unfolding behind the scenes, one that both curtailed the protests and coordinated the resistance from CEOs. Both surprises were the result of an informal alliance between left-wing activists and business titans. The pact was formalized in a terse, little-noticed joint statement of the U.S.

Chamber of Commerce and AFL-CIO published on Election Day. Both sides would come to see it as a sort of implicit bargain–inspired by the summer's massive, sometimes destructive racial-justice protests–in which the forces of labor came together with the forces of capital to keep the peace and oppose Trump's assault on democracy.

"The handshake between business and labor was just one component of a vast, cross-partisan campaign to protect the election–an extraordinary shadow effort dedicated not to winning the vote but to ensuring it would be free and fair, credible and uncorrupted." (sic)

In the topsy-turvy world of Leftist rhetoric, "to protect the election" and "ensuring it would be free and fair, credible and uncorrupted" meant that the wrong person—Donald J. Trump—was not declared the winner, regardless of the number of legal votes that might have been cast for him.

Again, in Ms. Ball's words, what happened in 2020 was:

"...a well-funded cabal of powerful people, ranging across industries and ideologies, working together behind the scenes to influence perceptions, change rules and laws, steer media coverage and control the flow of information. **They were not rigging the election; they were fortifying it."** *(Emphasis added)*

This Cabal was "fortifying" the election against the possibility that the people of America might vote to keep Donald Trump as President. Why would the Cabal do this? Because, as Hillary Clinton said, "We just can't trust the American people to make those types of choices".[2] In the minds of the Elites, the American people had made the wrong choice in 2016 when they rejected Her preordained ascension to the Presidency. By defying the wishes of the cabal in 2016, the American people proved themselves incapable of making the "right" choice. Thus, the need to "fortify" the election against another "wrong" choice by those Deplorables in the red hats.

Of course, as we know, the "fortification" worked. The will of the American people was ignored to insure their "wrong" choice was NOT allowed to continue in office for a second consecutive term.

Unfortunately for the Cabal, their efforts weren't as well-concealed as they would have liked. Despite the best efforts of those who conspired to "fortify" the 2020 election, as well as those who aided and abetted their efforts, more than half of likely American voters believe there was active cheating involved in the 2020 elections.[3] This includes 30 percent of Democrats, 51 percent of unaffiliated voters, and 75 percent of Republicans in this particular poll.

And because President Trump has begun seeking the Presidency again in 2024, he continues to be under attack from the same old enemies he has faced since 2015, with new ones piling on every day.

Some of these enemies are foreign nations, our adversaries who do not want Donald Trump to have a second term as President. These nations, chief among them China, would much rather have a weak President like Joe Biden. That Biden, and so many others, have been compromised and are complicit in helping China while enriching themselves at the expense of America, is an added benefit to the Chinese Communist Party and its leaders.[4]

It is understandable that China and other nations would support a weak American leader over a strong one—especially when that strong leader has a history of successfully promoting America First policies. It is, after all, how the Great Game is played. China desperately wants to be the world's Number One Power. To that end, China has been working for decades not only to build itself up but also to weaken the United States. Using Deng Xiaoping's "Hide and Bide"[5] strategy, infiltrating our institutions and industry, and subverting our leaders are just a few of the ways China has acted against America. That they have been so successful reflects well on them, and very poorly on us.

More insidious, and arguably more dangerous, are those attacks from America's "Enemies Domestic"—the Ruling Class Elites, their allies, apparatchiks, and useful idiots. Hardly a day goes by without yet another attack leveled against President Trump, then trumpeted (pun intended) in the media at every opportunity. More recently, there has been an increase in attacks against Trump and his supporters using the weaponized power of the U.S. Government. Perp walks of prominent Trump allies are now a common site on the evening news. The former President's Florida home was raided by the FBI. And, given the IRS's history of targeting conservatives under Obama, can we not expect the same to happen again? Why else would the Democrats more than double the size of the IRS by hiring 87,000 agents who must be "willing to use deadly force"?[6]

If you're concerned about that IRS expansion, and what it says about what's coming, you're not the only one. Michael Franzese has been concerned for some time about the Mafia-esque tactics our elected representatives have employed for years to enrich themselves and punish their enemies. Mr. Franzese, who at one time was a caporegime in the Colombo crime family in New York City, says:

> *"...I believe that's what is happening in America. Many of our government leaders are deceiving Americans into believing they are servants of the people, and in the process, they are enriching*

themselves at the people's expense and to the people's detriment. I can recognize Mafia-like behavior when I see it, and I am seeing a pattern of such behavior among leaders of our government today.

"America is not in the hands of patriots but rather in the grip of politicians who are gradually transforming America into a Mafia-style democracy."

—***Mafia Democracy: How Our Republic Became A Mob Racket****, Introduction*

From the mid-1970s until the mid-1990s, Mr. Franzese was a "made man" who rose through the Mafia ranks in one of New York's Five Families. He was eventually sent to prison by then-US Attorney for the Southern District of New York Rudi Guilliani, served nine years, and went on to become a successful author and friend to Mr. Guilliani.

Mafia Democracy is largely about how members of Congress get rich using mob-style schemes, but the recent pattern of thuggish politically-driven behavior by government agents and agencies makes drawing other parallels to the Mob all too easy. Faced with the overwhelming power and resources of the Department of Justice, the IRS, or the FBI, what hope does an average American have?

One can almost hear it now: "That's a nice little bank account you've got there. It'd be a shame if an audit happened to it."

Or: "Good morning! This is your 4:00 AM SWAT Team wake-up call!"

We can expect the "attention" of various agencies to be directed to MAGA leaders, especially those who begin to be more effective in standing up for MAGA-centric ideas. Until significant structural and cultural changes are made in how these agencies operate, the best we can do is actively support, in every possible way, those leaders as they endure the onslaught from the minions of the Regime.

Obviously, we will see more and more public attacks against President Trump, MAGA candidates for office, and MAGA Patriots in general from the Usual Suspects of the Enemies Domestic who wish to bring America to her knees. The relationships between these groups are complicated and often fluid. Some of them share considerable overlap in membership, especially as their goals of the moment overlap. Some of them are neutral or apathetic towards each other. For some, their relationship varies between antipathy and outright hatred. Nonetheless, they are united in the single-minded pursuit of a common goal: the destruction of that Great America envisioned by Donald J. Trump and his base.

Some of these most visible of the Usual Suspects include:

- The Sufferers of the Sins of the Father
- The Angsty Academics and the Irate Intelligentsia
- The Screeching Socialists and the Pontificating Progressives
- The Status Quo Deep Staters
- The NGO Zombies
- The Neo-Clowns of the Empire of Eternal War
- The Globalist Ghouls
- The Tech Lords of the Interwebz
- And of course, the Uniparty Establishment

The Suffers of the Sins of the Father are those who devoutly believe the version of history presented in the 1619 Project.[7] According to their Marxist-derived dogma, America is forever tainted by the

Original Sin of slavery and its sequela, systemic racism. No matter what has been done to rectify this, the stain of slavery will never be removed from the nation (but a huge cash payout would be nice). Destroying America, by escalating racial tension and stigmatizing "whiteness",[8] is to their way of thinking the only possible course of action. That there might be reasons other than systemic racism for the failure of certain ethnic groups to do as well as others is an unspeakable heresy. That Trump's economic policies benefited blacks, as well as whites,[9] is a mere distraction, if not an outright lie[10] to the Sufferers.

The Angsty Academics and the Irate Intelligentsia and their fellow travelers outside the Ivory Towers, the Screeching Socialists and the Pontificating Progressives, are those highly-(over)educated Marx-loving Elites who are upset that the rest of the nation not only fails to realize their obvious superiority[11] but refuses to let them dictate every facet of their lives. Whether they are Fabianist followers,[12] frustrated Frankfurters,[13] or the inventors of their own unique idiotology,[14] they are angry that their utopian schemes[15] haven't been implemented. Or, their plans have been tried, and failed miserably, as Marxian schemes always do. They are far gone into the Destructionist Stage[16] of their millenarian intellectual movement(s). Fortunately for them, their shame at having their lovely theories repudiated by cold, unfeeling reality has a ready target—it becomes rage at that evil man Trump and his equally evil MAGA people. Faced with either admitting to themselves they might have been wrong or burning the country to the ground, they've chosen the psychologically easy path—burn it all down!

The Status Quo Deep Staters are those tens of thousands of bureaucrats who were directly threatened[17] by President Trump's Schedule F Executive Order. Faced with the very real possibility that they might actually have to be accountable for their work performance,[18] they no doubt worked hard in 2020 to see Trump defeated. Since Second-Term (Third Win) Trump will undoubtedly pursue Schedule F vigorously as part of an overall plan to Drain the Swamp,[19] their ongoing resistance to any MAGA candidate can be assumed.

Similarly, the Non-Governmental Organization (NGO) Zombies are deeply invested in the status quo. A sprawling collection of think tanks, nonprofits, and charitable trusts centered around the wealth of the Capital,[20] they exist to move money in and out,[21] push and pull policy[22] and in general see to it that the government always grows. The general MAGA objective of shrinking government and reducing its influence on everyone's daily lives makes the NGOs MAGA's natural enemies.

The Neo-Clowns[23] of the Empire of Eternal War and the Globalist Ghouls[24] have spent decades replacing the British Empire with the American Empire. Presently, they have imposed a proxy war with Russia (and possibly China—they never think small) on America and Europe, and are working towards their Great Reset.[25] They desire nothing less than complete domination of the world, by any means necessary. Listen to what the Elites say at gatherings of the World Economic Forum, or read the policies that seem to flow so endlessly from Davos[26] or the minds of the Council on Foreign Relations or Trilateral Commission. They have passed the point of bothering to conceal their plans from the plebes they intend to rule over.[27] Donald Trump's remarkable record of being the only President in many years to NOT start a war while in office is a direct affront to their sensibilities and to the Military-Industrial Complex's profits. Their resistance to his America First policy then, now and in the future can be taken as a given.

Aside from their liberal bent,[28] the Tech Lords of the Interwebz hate and despise Donald Trump because he seized one of their platforms and used it to mercilessly troll their Lefty users all the way to the White House. He showed them up and mocked them and their friends while doing it. That Lefties can't meme worth a damn was just icing on the cake for those on the Right, and using the Tech Lord's own tools to spread them (and make snowflakes melt down on a regular basis) continues to irritate them no end. Because of this, the Tech Lords and their Deep State allies,[29] especially Daddy Zuckerbucks,[30] were actively involved in "fortifying" the 2020 election,[31] and steps were taken[32] to do the same in 2022 (and probably 2024). The rise of alternate platforms—Gab, GETTR, Truth Social and FrankSpeech, specifically—to directly compete with the Tech Lords only assures their continued animosity towards any and all conservatives, especially MAGA users.

Finally, we come to the One Big Uniparty Establishment.[33] As has been said, "it's a big club, and you ain't in it."[34] Regardless of the letters attached to their names, a large number of our "leaders" have much more in common with each other than they ever did with the people who elected them.[35] For some, this was their initial goal in seeking high office. For others, the corrosive nature of the Washington atmosphere has taken what were initially honest (well, as far as politicians go) men and women and corrupted them.[36] Perhaps it's prolonged exposure to all that marble that changes their brains? Who can say? Whatever the reason(s), it's obvious—between the Democrats and the RINOs and Never-Trumpers, it's clear that President Trump and MAGA Patriots have precious few friends inside the Washington Beltway.

The ongoing attacks on President Trump and MAGA Patriots from our Enemies Domestic have only one true purpose: to stop the man and the movement from restoring the Constitutional Republic envisioned by the Founders of this great nation. Whatever their stated reasons, motivations, and excuses, the enemies of MAGA desire nothing less than the destruction of these United States. That said destruction also entails destroying those of us who still believe in silly old ideas like Truth, Justice, and "the American Way" is to them a feature, not a bug.

The Enemies Domestic want to tear down the original meaning and intent of the Constitution and the just laws it supports. They want to unwind the Declaration of Independence, eliminating those unalienable rights, endowed by the Creator, which this government was created to secure. They want to undo the radical notion that a People can choose to govern themselves directly, without a divine chain of authority flowing down through princes or prelates, and without needing the permission of their betters in the Ruling Class.

They want to erase from the world any memory of a great nation of self-governing People, and the incredible things that nation was able to do because those People chose to do great things.

They want to destroy the idea of America—"that shining city on the hill", that "torch that enlightens the entire world". They are determined that the very concept of a government of, by, and for the People shall utterly perish from this earth.

Given the large number of domestic enemies the MAGA Movement faces, MAGA Patriots must be aware of both the mindset and tactics that will be used against them. Most Patriots are already familiar with many of them from first-hand experience. For those who are not, count your blessings—you've been lucky thus far!

For everyone else, or for when your luck runs out, Hansen's **The Case for Trump** lays out the mindset that drives the Left:

> *"The coastal blue states, in the manner of Athenian arrogance in dismissing Spartan parochialism, often believed they were*

winning the cultural wars. Sometimes the blue mindset grew haughty, and insisted that no quarter should be given. In a widely quoted and disseminated essay in the online blog Medium in early 2018, progressives Peter Leyden (founder and CEO of Reinvent) and Ray Teixeira (fellow at the Center for American Progress) saw the divide as existential, permanent, and intractable. They urged liberals to take no prisoners. And they were clear about the need to defeat and eliminate rather than compromise with their enemies:

"The opportunity for compromise is then lost. This is where America is today… At some point, one side or the other must win—and win big. The side resisting change, usually the one most rooted in the past systems and incumbent interests, must be thoroughly defeated—not just for a political cycle or two, but for a generation or two."

Such take-no-prisoners boasts were updated in July 2019 by MSNBC anchor Chris Hayes. Without much shame, Hayes advocated destroying the Trump base ("the darkness")—although he conceded annihilating them with his version of love and compassion:

"It [the Trump constituency] must be peacefully, nonviolently, politically destroyed with love, compassion, and determination, but utterly confronted and destroyed. That is the only way to break the coalition apart. Not by prying off this or that interest. They are in too deep. They have shamed themselves too much. The heart of the thing must be ripped out. The darkness must be banished."

> *The divide in which some "must be thoroughly defeated" or, rather, "destroyed" and "ripped out" always sharpened...."*
>
> —***The Case for Trump***, Ch. 1

For the MAGA Movement to successfully challenge the Left, much less have any hope of defeating them and restoring the Republic, the Left will have to be met head-on, on equal terms. Those who are unwilling to "fight fire with fire"—to confront the Left at every turn, with the same energy, enthusiasm, and determination to win—are not allies who can be trusted in this fight.

This does NOT mean that MAGA Patriots should have the same disregard for the rule of law and social order as the comrades of the Left—far from it. It does, however, mean that the days of (alleged) Republicans making a token showing as the "loyal opposition", before folding like a cheap umbrella in a hurricane, are OVER.

Painful experience has taught us that the bow tie-wearing, silk-stockinged Country Club Elites of Cuckservative, Inc. are as much our enemies as Antifa, the Squad, and the Tides Foundation. We've learned the hard way that:

- There's no advantage to holding the moral high ground against people with no morals
- Turning the other cheek guarantees you'll be slapped twice
- Saying "we're better than that" means you've already surrendered without a fight
- Saying you "refuse to sink to their level" only works if you can walk on water

President Trump is so effective and so beloved by MAGA Patriots because he gives back to the Left exactly what the Left gives out, and they simply can not handle it. He'll certainly continue to do so, and it should empower MAGA Patriots to do the same.

It's time (and long past) for MAGA Patriots to give the Left a taste of their own medicine, call them out on their little tricks, and give them the same consideration they give their opponents—none.

In other words:

- NO quarter
- NO compromise
- NO surrender

If MAGA Patriots are not willing to engage the Left directly, on an equal footing, with similar rules of engagement, the fight is already lost. Any chance to salvage, much less restore the Republic in the months and years to come will dwindle away to nothing. The trajectory of the country's decline will not change, and the nation will sink further into that "fundamental transformation" Obama promised.

MAGA Patriots should NEVER use, much less endorse the blatantly illegal activities the Left often adapts—the rampant fraud committed in the 2020 election being just the most obvious example. Nor should MAGA Patriots engage in anything as destructive as the "mostly peaceful protests"[37] of the Burn Loot Mobs. These "mostly peaceful protests"[38] were not merely uncivilized. They were actively ANTIcivilized—acts directly against, and counter to, civil society. The Left's failure to immediately condemn them[39] and the peripheral violence[40] they spawned was sadly unsurprising.

MAGA Patriots, don't SAY "we're better than that"—SHOW IT with how you act. And when the Burn Loot Mobs come? Just remember, the defense of self, others, and property are some of the most important reasons we have the Second Amendment.

For conservatives in general and MAGA Patriots in particular, what's desperately needed is an attitude of "Failure is NOT an option". Leftists never admit defeat. They never publicly back down. They demand complete, total, and abject surrender to their demands, and will push any form of compromise to its limits, and then some. They are absolutely convinced of the virtues of their cause and refuse to consider any other options.

The Left are bullies, and they hate Donald Trump because he stands up to them and isn't cowed by their antics.

MAGA Patriots need to accept that history really is on our side. Progressivism, socialism, communism, call it what you will, always lead to misery for the common man and woman. These ideologies always fall short of their glorious promises, and always fail. Witness what happened under eight years of Obama, and only two years under Biden—scandal piled on calamity heaped with failure. Remind a Democrat about that record and they'll lie, deny and attack you because they have no other way to answer, except to admit you are correct. And, they can not allow themselves to do that.

Ultimately, their lies, denials, and attacks don't matter, because MAGA Patriots know the truth. Just as important, so do the vast majority of young Independents, who are roughly as numerous as Democrats and Republicans, combined.[41] Rest assured, they are watching....

Beating back the Left doesn't require MAGA Patriots to lie, cheat and steal at every opportunity. Leave that to the Democrats—God knows they have enough practice at it.

What Patriots must be willing to do is use every angle, every legal option, and every resource available to support MAGA goals while undermining the Progressive agenda. After all, Isn't that what the Left has been doing to conservatives for decades?

MAGA Patriots need to be unafraid to call the Left out—long, loud, and in public—every time they try their usual shenanigans. Insist that Lefties follow the law and play by the rules. Remind them that fair is fair. Demand exactly the same standards and restrictions for all parties. When they use the bureaucracy to tie things in knots, learn to play that game and beat them at that, too. Match them at every step. Refuse to give up or be worn down. Keep reminding them that history itself is against them (they REALLY hate that!). Do this every time, and most of their victories can be turned into their defeats.

In other words, make things as miserable and difficult for them as they delight in making things for you. Remember, your mantra must be:

- NO quarter
- NO compromise
- NO surrender

Stand up to the bullies of the Left correctly, calmly, and consistently and they will absolutely fall apart. They have little experience with people who they can't intimidate or browbeat, and they aren't able to tolerate frustration when it's turned back on them. What's more, doing it above board and honestly will only make the frustration worse.

Former California State Senator H.L. Richardson recommends the following when dealing with the Left:

"...we should analyze their weaknesses and look for vulnerabilities. We should probe their mistakes, find their Achilles' heel and use the issue to find new allies who just had their hot button pushed. Then, we must influence them into joining the fight, registering to vote, and contributing to the cause."

—**Confrontational Politics**, *Ch. 15*

Every point of contention, every conflict with those on the Left is an opportunity to frustrate them and roll back their agenda. It's also the chance to recruit others into the MAGA Movement. Recruiting others to support America First ideals is the surest path to victory, and should always be kept in mind. Remember, all those young Independents are watching….

As much as it should be otherwise, the Establishment RINOs will continue to be troublesome opponents of the MAGA Movement. They are the most likely culprits (aside from stealth Alphabet Agents[42]—everybody wave at Ray Epps![43]) to infiltrate MAGA and try to destroy it from within. They've done it before with the Tea Party, and they will again. External attacks are always easier to spot and defend against than those that come from inside any group, in part because outside attacks are expected. It's the knife in the back from the so-called friend that's so difficult to anticipate and defend against.

Rank-and-file little-c conservatives have tried (and tried, and tried, and tried) to resist the Left for decades by listening to the alleged "leaders" of the Conservative movement, and look where it's gotten us. Losses on every front, in every major battle. Those few minor victories we've been allowed to have repeatedly held up as examples of just how "effective" the Establishment RINOs and Conservative, Inc. have been.

Perhaps the best example of just how "effective" a RINO, card-carrying member of Conservative, Inc. can be at (not) acting like a conservative came on July 28th, 2017. Arizona Senator John "Songbird" McCain voted 'NO' with double thumbs down to defeat Republicans' long-promised repeal and replacement of Obamacare. Whether it was purely to spite Donald J. Trump, or for some other reason is immaterial at this point. The facts are that for years, Republicans repeatedly promised to repeal and replace Obamacare. When it was finally about to become a reality, John McCain (joined by perennial weak sisters Lisa Murkowski of Alaska and Susan Collins of Maine) saved Obamacare[44] in the wee hours of a Friday morning.

McCain was literally dying at the time, having left his hospital bed to return to cap his too-long career in the Senate with this slap in the face to President Trump and the Republican rank and file. It epitomized his career as a pure creature of the DC Swamp and is one of the main reasons his name is invoked as an example of what a MAGA Patriot ought NOT to be.

A major goal of MAGA must always be to guard against neo-McCains, whenever and wherever they appear. If a leader is elected by espousing MAGA principles, then they should be expected to follow those principles once in office. If they do not—then at the earliest opportunity, they should be replaced with a MAGA leader who will follow MAGA principles consistently.

This is why every election cycle matters. In every election, MAGA Patriots must be willing to take a long, hard look at their representatives at every level and ask if those representatives have supported causes and issues that are consistent with MAGA and America First principles. If yes, then they should be supported. If not? Then their MAGA constituency should have no reluctance to remove and replace them with someone who WILL actively support the MAGA agenda.

As daunting as the task may seem, there is still hope that the Republic may be saved. The MAGA Movement is growing in strength every day. MAGA Patriots are highly energized and motivated. America First citizens are rallying behind strong pro-America First leaders. And finally, we have something which the Left entirely lacks: a sense of humor.

The Left, especially the radical Progressives who have effectively seized control of the Democratic Party, have ZERO defense against humor, satire, irony, and memes because they are without any sense of humor themselves. They frequently are not smart enough to know when they're being purposefully trolled, as President Trump has proved time and time again.

Our 45th President is the Grand Master of this. Learn from him well, you must, MAGA padawans.

If you're a MAGA Patriot and you haven't yet learned to meme[45], ask a fellow Patriot for some to share. Swap Libtard jokes whenever possible. Never be afraid to laugh at them, because it's impossible to laugh WITH a Libtard.

The ascendancy of America First ideas, the MAGA Movement, and the restoration of the Republic will not be an act so much as it will be a process. Acts must follow acts, followed by still more acts. Rinse, wash, repeat; over and over again. There will be losses, yes; they cannot be allowed to bog down the Movement. Victories must follow both losses and other victories, and these victories cannot be allowed to slow down the Movement, either. There can be no resting upon any laurels if MAGA is to succeed.

Most important of all: each election cycle must be won anew if we are to triumph against our always-active foes.

The enemies of MAGA will never be completely defeated short of the Final Trump (pun intended), which is why we must train future MAGA leaders to revere and cherish our Founders, our liberties, our freedoms, and the price those freedoms require from each of us every day.

Above all else, keep in mind the final words of the Declaration of Independence:

"...with a firm Reliance on the Protection of Divine Providence, we mutually pledge to each other our Lives, our Fortunes, and our sacred Honor."

In those words lies the key to MAGA's victory.

FIVE

2024 Is Coming

"When you can't make them see the light, make them feel the heat."—Ronald Reagan

WE ARE FACING A "LIVES, *fortunes and sacred Honor" moment. The situation is dire, but we cannot afford to fall into despair. We are not alone—over 70 million Patriots stand together, and failure is NOT an option! We must lay the groundwork for 2024 by ensuring election integrity. We must elect and support MAGA leaders and insist that they stay true to MAGA principles. We must increase MAGA's influence at state and local levels, push an America First agenda in Congress, and replace progressive school boards with MAGA Patriots. We need to have recall procedures in every State to remove leaders who stand against America's interests as we begin unwinding the toxic policies of the Left. Restoring the Republic is a marathon, not a sprint. MAGA Patriots must address our issues at all levels, seek out allies, and never stop pressing forward. 2024 is coming!*

. . .

"…OUR Lives, our Fortunes, and our sacred Honor."

Our People and our Nation are in a "Lives, Fortunes and sacred Honor" moment.

The situation is dire. The sheer number of issues that must be addressed to return the county to the Republic created by the Founders is overwhelming. So many things have to be fixed, against such strongly entrenched opposition, that it's easy to fall into despair. It seems like an impossible task, and it would be—for any one person or small group. Fortunately, it won't come to that.

You may be just one person. You and your friends may be just a small group. But, you are NOT alone! You (and your friends) are in some of the best company imaginable, and you have 70+ million friends and fellow Patriots who are in the fight with you.

Hundreds, if not thousands of small groups have already sprung up, each dealing with their own piece of the elephant.[1] That's how the radical Left was able to make so much progress—one step at a time, over months, years, and decades. That's how MAGA Patriots are pushing back with the America First agenda—one step, one issue, one outrage at a time, for as many months, years, and decades as are needed. Taken as a whole, the nation's problems are nigh insurmountable. Broken down into manageable pieces, it becomes just a matter of putting in the time and effort to address each issue.

The MAGA Movement will win because it must—failure is NOT an option.

MAGA Patriots will need to accomplish a number of things in the near term, the most important being laying the groundwork for success in the 2024 election. This will primarily involve issues dealing with election integrity. Another "fortified" election like 2020 will likely see the country damaged beyond all hope of repair.

What will happen if 2024 is a repeat of 2020 is something I shudder to contemplate, and no sensible person wants to test.

At the national level, supporting an America First agenda in Congress, especially MAGA and pro-MAGA Representatives and Senators who stand up to the Biden et. al. Regime is critically important. The MAGA Movement must increase its influence in Congress. The Congressional election cycle mandates, for all practical purposes, that the House and Senate be retaken every two years. It is not enough to "take and hold" Congress for the Republican (or any other) party. The power of the Swamp to corrupt and seduce even the most devoted patriots can not be underestimated.[2] The nation can no longer tolerate leaders who are elected promising to support MAGA but promptly turn into John McCains.

We saw an excellent example of assertive MAGA influence in the kerfuffle over the Speaker's position in the 118th Congress in January, 2023. This little bit of "Pitchfork Populism"[3] was decried by all and sundry at the time. But, by standing strong on their principles the Freedom 20 were able to leverage significant concessions out of the eventual Speaker. Despite the new Speaker not embracing pro-MAGA, pro-America First candidates in 2022,[4] the possibility he wouldn't achieve the Speakership he so desperately craved[5] forced him to accept many of the Freedom 20's demands.[6]

Once elected, Congressional leaders should be expected to stay true to their campaign promises, and if elected as MAGA candidates they should act and vote as MAGA leaders. If they do not, then their MAGA constituents should recall or replace them as soon as possible, and choose another, better MAGA leader in their stead.

"MAGA-izing" Congress won't be accomplished in a single cycle. To be frank, it will never be finished. Some Swamp Critters will hide in the mud even after the Swamp has been drained. The Left has spent decades moving the country in its chosen direction. Restoring the Republic won't be accomplished overnight. This is a marathon, not a sprint; be patient, and never stop working to preserve our rights and freedoms.

This "marathon, not sprint" mentality is essential to the long-term success of the MAGA Movement. Without it, the inevitable losses that will be suffered along the way could demoralize and destroy the Movement—and with it, any hope of saving, much less restoring America.

This is for all the marbles, kiddies. If MAGA fails, the light of liberty will go out for decades or more, and the dark times so fervently desired by America's enemies will fall on her citizens, her children, and the world.

President Trump called America "the Torch that Enlightens the entire World".[7] Should that torch be extinguished, the world will fall into shadows from which it may never fully recover. This is why MAGA and the America First agenda must succeed, and why engaging—and winning—the political process is so critically important.

Once MAGA candidates begin to win (honest) elections, those MAGA leaders can begin unwinding the toxic, unworkable policies of the Left. Leading up to the 2024 elections, MAGA leaders in Congress must do everything possible to frustrate the plans of the Biden administration and Congressional Democrats. This will mean using every means available, especially the Power of the Purse, to begin undoing the last two years of damage to the economy, the military, the border, the energy sector, manufacturing, shipping… basically everything.

If anyone can think of something, anything Brandon and his pit crew haven't wrecked, please let me know. I honestly can't think of anything they've touched that they haven't ruined.

There are two schools of thought on how MAGA Representatives and Senators can stand against Biden, Harris, Pelosi, Schumer, and all the rest.

One school is that MAGA leaders in Congress should move carefully, pick their battles, and only apply their maximum leverage and efforts sparingly when the issue is truly important or victory is assured.

The other option is to hit the halls of Congress like BLM hits a Nike® store. Refuse to accept the dictates of the Establishment about how things are "supposed" to work. Disrupt "business as usual" at every opportunity. Be as loud and intransigent as the Progressives have been since The Squad was first elected. Refuse to be cowed. Never be shy about letting the American People know what you're being threatened with, and by whom, if you don't sit down, shut up and stop making waves.

We need more waves made in the Swamp. That's why we're sending MAGA Representatives up there—to make those waves! Yes, making waves will bring threats from all sides with loss of power, loss of privileges, loss of access to money, and every other perk. When the threats come, as they will: document them, record them, share them; let the People know. 2024 Is Coming....

The first option—the slow, careful, timid option—will make it easier to work with non-MAGA Republicans and within the existing system. While it won't be as fast as many would like, it has the advantage of letting MAGA members claim at least a few victories in the run-up to 2024.

In other words, business as usual.

Thank you, no. That way lies McCain-dom.

Look at what the Progressives have done with their no-holds-barred approach. From four members of the Squad[8] to over ninety members admitting to being in the Congressional Progressive Caucus in a bit over three years is remarkable! It's even more remarkable when you consider the competence (read: severe lack thereof) of their first members[9] and the fact that their policies range from the idiotic to the floridly delusional.

Disconnected from reality and dumb as a box of rocks most Progressives may be, they know how to work with the (admittedly, very supportive) press to cover up their slips and push their agenda forward. They've done it not with facts (which they don't have) but with constant engagement with the feelings and emotions of their base. They have terrorized their supporters and colleagues[10] with portents of certain doom if they weren't heeded—12 years to save the planet, wasn't it?[11]—and being absolutely immovable on their issues.

I dream of the day when there are more than just a handful of America Firsters in Congress fighting just as hard on behalf of 70 million (and more every day[12]) MAGA Patriots. Yes, I know that there are more than just a handful, but some days it seems like there are only a few.

Duplicating the success of the Progressive Caucus will be difficult because MAGA will be fighting not only the "regular" Dems and rabid Progressives but also the Mainstream Media, the RINOs and the Swamp itself. However, MAGA has one very clear advantage in this fight!

America First policies have been proven to work during President Trump's first term, and the People remember it. That is a record that the Progressives can't hope to dismiss.

Inflation. The economy. Immigration and the border. Crime. Afghanistan and now Ukraine. On the issues most Americans care about, the America First policies of Donald J. Trump worked, and worked well. In contrast, Biden's Green Raw Deal energy policies, lead-from-behind foreign policy, southern invasion immigration policy—it's all been a disaster, and now it's snowballing.

It's likely we'll be not just in a recession,[13] but an undeniable, Big-D Depression[14],[15] sometime in 2023. Changing the definition one more time won't take away the pain Americans are feeling now, and will be feeling more over the next many months. If or when that happens, every MAGA leader, activist and influencer at every level has to make sure every voter knows just whose fault it is.

Hint: NOT Donald J. Trump!

Given the continuing deterioration of the economy[16] and the willful blindness and total disconnect from Flyover America the Establishment has embraced for years, MAGA Patriots in Congress and elsewhere need to band together to deliver a strong, unified, consistent message.

That message? It's simple:

> *The Biden administration and the Establishment caused this mess. Remember how well the economy did under President Trump? We can use those same ideas now to begin fixing things, if Biden and the Dems will just cooperate.*

Push that message relentlessly. Hammer home just how bad Biden's idiocy has made things, and how quickly they've fallen apart.

> *Remember good growth, full shelves, low inflation, cheaper gas? Remember when we had enough energy? Remember when we didn't need rolling brown-outs or 'no-charge, no cooking, no cleaning, no laundry, no power' times?*
>
> *Wouldn't it be nice to have all that back?*
>
> *We can, you know. 2024 is coming….*

While America First leaders in Washington are pushing back against the Regime, grassroots efforts at both State and local levels that have already started must accelerate. This begins with ensuring 2020-level election fraud does NOT happen in 2024. The Democrats cannot be allowed to have eight full years to inflict the same level of disastrous, destructive policies on the nation as they've done since Biden was placed in the Oval Office. If they do, there won't be much of the country left to save.

Insuring the integrity of our elections is primarily a state-level task. While these efforts naturally need strong support at the national level, how we elect our leaders is a matter for the States to decide. With 2024 rapidly approaching, this is arguably the single most important thing MAGA Patriots must do. Everything else must—MUST—take a back seat to election integrity.

Election integrity must be the first priority in every State. Period. Full stop.

In a perfect world, this wouldn't be an issue in the first place. In a slightly less perfect world, there would be unlimited resources to draw on to address every single issue at once. In this world, the reality is that there are only so many MAGA Patriots to go around, and their time, energy, money and influence are finite. Hard choices will be made and priorities will be set.

Some may not agree with this, but consider this: if Leftist politicians are able to steal elections at will, what will they do?

Hint: they won't push America First, MAGA-centric policies.

As tough as it will be to clean up our elections then win with pro-MAGA candidates, it is ultimately the easiest, most effective path to the widespread adoption of constitutional conservative policies. Instead of constantly fighting a bunch of progressive, woke Marxists on the (insert commission/board/committee here), why not just elect reasonable leaders to start with?

School Boards are an excellent example of this tactic already being put into practice. Newly-awakened and irritated parents have already won school board elections for common-sense, conservative candidates in a number of states. There is every reason to believe this trend will continue as local and municipal election cycles allow. Taking back school boards is the first step towards taking back the nation's education system, and it's being done at the ballot box.

The Progressive domination of academia and the educational system is under siege by parent groups all across the country. The Powers That Be completely underestimated the effects that lockdowns would have on parent's awareness of what their children were being taught. Lockdowns made parents aware of what was being presented to their children, and those parents did NOT like it.

Parents who went to their School Boards protesting Social Emotional Learning, Critical Race Theory, Gender Acceptance, and Diversity, Equity, Inclusion programs caused the Educrats to petition Biden's Department of Justice for relief. In a critical blunder by the Regime, Attorney General Merrick Garland responded in typical statist fashion. He declared these parents "domestic terrorists".[17]

This was THE Red Pill Moment for many parents. They thought they were being good parents by becoming involved in their child's education. Isn't this what educators always say they want? Apparently not, since vigorously objecting to what their tax dollars were paying for at school board meetings landed these parents on FBI watch lists.[18]

Despite Garland's frantic backpedaling,[19] the damage has already been done.[20] Educrats and School Board members are learning just why you don't threaten a mama bear's cubs, and you don't threaten a mama bear when she's defending her cubs.[21]

Academia fell to the radical, Marxist Left, over many decades. Given the nature of tenure and faculty politics, it will take at least a decade to begin to see any appreciable change. One way to do that is already happening—replacing Leftist School Board members with MAGA Patriots—and this trend must continue. Only by de-electing Progressive School Boards (or the people who appoint them) can Critical Race Theory, Grooming under the guise of Diversity, Inclusion and Equity, Social-Emotional Learning, and all their derivatives be removed from our schools. These corrosive ideologies are more than inappropriate for our children—they are actively harmful, anti-social, and anti-liberty.[22] They are tools being used to prepare our children for more Marxist indoctrination in colleges and universities or to accept Marxist narratives as promulgated by the mainstream media.

Sunlight truly is the best disinfectant, and shining a light on exactly what is being taught from kindergarten onward is the best first step to take in ridding our schools of the toxicity that is Marxist Progressivism. If there is a silver lining to the COVID cloud, forcing schools to close forced parents to pay attention to what their kids were doing with their home-based learning. Obviously, parents did NOT like what they saw. This is the reason homeschool numbers jumped significantly during the past two years, and there is no indication they will be coming down anytime soon.

That parents and kids are interacting more as a family over their lessons is a welcome benefit to an otherwise disastrous policy. The same can be said for the growing interest in "backpack funding"[23] and other school choice programs across the nation.

Another State-level MAGA focus needs to be directed towards establishing recall procedures for elected leaders, especially Senators and Representatives. This will allow States to remove those leaders, Democrat and RINO, who continue to work against MAGA, without waiting for the next election cycle. This is especially needed for long-term Senators who shall not be named but are a large part of the problem. These fossils have tremendous advantages in seeking re-election, and then the country is stuck with them for another 6 (or 60) years.

Election to Congress shouldn't be a life sentence. It's time certain people were reminded of that.

Having the ability to recall every elected official, at every level, gives power back to the People and provides the ultimate check against corrupt behavior in office.

Yes, there should be some common-sense limits on how often recalls can be initiated. Yes, they are difficult and expensive to hold. The answer to these objections is simple: do you want to live in a Republic? Or, in a feudal system with nobles and serfs? Without term limits, with the ability of incumbents to tap special interest money and all their other advantages, aren't long-term Congresscum de facto nobles already?

Some years ago I was told that the turnover rate of the British House of Lords was higher than the United States Senate. It would not surprise me in the least if it were true, then and now.

It goes without saying that the integrity of these recall elections is as important as any other.

Election integrity, local education, and recall movements are just a few of the issues to be addressed at the State and local level. MAGA Patriots have much to do before the 2024 election; but remember, you are not alone. Seek out your friends and neighbors, join with them, and never stop pressing forward.

2024 Is Coming!

SIX

Maga: 2024 And Beyond

"It does not take a majority to prevail... but rather an irate, tireless minority, keen on setting brushfires of freedom in the minds of men."—Samuel Adams

THE 2024 ELECTION *truly is the most important of our lifetime. Another four years of Biden's disastrous policies, sheer incompetence, insane spending and woke wackiness may not leave us a country to save. If America First candidates win the White House and Congress, the country can return to policies of national security, sovereignty, and economic nationalism that worked so well during President Trump's first term. In his next term, President Trump's vision for America includes restoring national support for our police, making our streets safer, and aggressively targeting organized criminal gangs. He also plans to restore the economy, eliminate the Green New Deal, return America to energy independence, and eliminate Marxist, woke dogma from our children's education. He will protect our Constitutional right* to self-defense, ensure the integrity of our elections, rebuild our infrastructure, and address the national debt. He will promote American energy, enact tax reform, and encourage American corporations to make major investments in the US. Finally, President Trump will work to reduce violent crime, substantially upgrade all aspects of the military, and promote peace through strength. Trump's plan to rebuild the economy and undo the damage done by Biden's handlers is aggressive and active, and we can follow it on his campaign website, Truth Social and other platforms, and his Rumble channel.

It's cliche to say that every election is "the most important in our lifetime" but in 2024 the cliche is also the ugly reality.

Consider the difference between America at the end of 2019 and after less than two years of the Biden Regime. Remember how relatively calm the world was in 2019, as opposed to early 2023? Assuming the nukes haven't flown by November 2024–and that's by no means a safe assumption—what will America be like at that time?

Do this thought experiment: run the trends since early 2021 forward in your mind. Extrapolate the results of a full four years of:

- More incompetence from the Dementoid in Chief
- More ridiculous policies to satisfy the various delusions of the Left's fractious factions
- More insane spending to further wreck the economy and devalue the dollar
- More woke wackiness, enforced by the unrestrained, politicized Alphabet Agencies of a government weaponized against its people

Not a very pretty picture, is it? Even then, what we can imagine is almost certainly a pale shadow of what the reality will be should the Left keep control of the country in 2024. What will be left of America in 2028? 2032?

The most important election of our lives, indeed.

Now do another thought experiment: assume that we still have something resembling a country in late 2024, and America First candidates dedicated to Making America Great Again take the White House and at least one chamber of Congress.

What happens then?

As President Trump told his audience at CPAC 2022:[1]

> *"We cannot be complacent. We have to seize this opportunity to deal with the radical left socialist lunatics and fascists. And we have to hit them very, very hard. Has to be a crippling defeat, because our country cannot take it.*
>
> *"We have to take this chance to shatter the corrupt Washington establishment once and for all. We have to run aggressive, unrelenting, and boldly, populist campaigns. Populist. We want to be populist. We want to love our country. That's what we want."*
>
> *We have to throw off the shackles of globalism, and reassert two very important words. You know what the words are? America First."*

America First.

Two words that have defined Trump's political philosophy since he began his campaign. Two words that lay at the heart of the policies of the first Trump administration and will drive the agenda of a second Trump term.

At CPAC 2017,[2] Steve Bannon spoke about the "three verticals" the Trump White House was "laser-focused" on in its first few months:

- national security and sovereignty
- economic nationalism
- deconstruction of the administrative state

Putting America First with this intense focus on national security, sovereignty and economic nationalism resulted in one of the most rapid economic transformations in history. Within months, the anemic, moribund Obama economy became an engine of vibrant, rapid growth.[3] Within two years of Trump's inauguration, America became energy independent for the first time in nearly 70 years[4] and was rapidly moving into a position of energy dominance. Growth shot up, as did job creation. Regulations eased, which benefited businesses, especially small businesses. Inflation remained low, while consumer confidence climbed. The man who literally wrote the book on *The Art of the Deal* undid NAFTA and many other trade agreements that disadvantaged America, and replaced them with far, far better arrangements.

Since the country is arguably worse off after just over two years of Sleepy Joe than it ever was under Obama, it's virtually certain that by Inauguration Day 2025 we will be in very bad shape indeed. The next President will have to work long and hard just to undo the damage Biden's handlers have done and return to where we were in January 2021. Sadly, this may take more than a single term because Biden's policies have been so thoroughly disastrous in so many areas, both at home and abroad. We can only pray that returning to America First policies in January 2025 is enough to avert the inevitable train wreck that Biden & Co. are working so hard to arrange.[5]

At the 2022 America First PAC,[6] the 2022 Conservative Political Action Coalition (CPAC)[7] Conventions, and at his Mar-A-Lago Campaign Announcement[8] President Trump highlighted a number of issues and his solutions to the problems related to those issues. Taken together, these three speeches provide a glimpse of what we can expect from a second Trump administration.

Above all, as President Trump said at Mar-A-Lago, "Our victory will be built upon big ideas, bold ambitions and daring dreams for America's future. We need daring dreams." His vision, and ours, for America is big, bold and daring—in a word, "great". Not for us the petty, small-minded, self- and country-loathing policies of the Left. Inherent in President Trump's platform and the entire MAGA, America First movement is the bone-deep conviction that America can be, should be and will be great—despite the best efforts of the Left!

Focusing initially on Public Safety, because "If we don't have safety, we don't have freedom, we don't have a country. America first must mean safety first. We have to have safety,"[9] President Trump laid out his ambitious plans, not only to return to the policies of his previous administration but to reverse the corrosive, America Last policies of the Biden regime.

Acknowledging that "The list of urgent tasks for the next Congress and the next President is endless and we do not have (time) to wait. We have to move quickly,"[10] President Trump shared his vision for restoring national support for our police, making our cities and streets safer, and aggressively targeting organized gangs, especially those involved in the drug trade. He spoke about the need to reverse Biden's open borders immigration policies that have been so destructive. He promised to resume the previous administration's policies that had been working so well to curb the flow of illegals into our country.

The President also addressed the need to restore our economy, eliminate the Green New Deal and return America to energy independence, continue bringing our supply chains and manufacturing back to our shores, eliminate Marxist, woke dogma from our children's education, restore the welfare work requirement, protect our Constitutional right to self-defense, and ensure the integrity of our elections.

Since the President's Mar-A-Lago announcement he has launched DonaldJTrump.com, his campaign website. He continues to post frequently on Truth Social, and his Rumble channel hosts videos of his rallies and major policy announcements. There can be no doubt that the President has an active, aggressive agenda and plan to rebuild our economy and undo the damage Joe Biden's handlers have done to our nation.

At CPAC[11] on March 4, 2023, President Trump gave a major address that laid out, in no uncertain terms, exactly what he will do as our 47th President. Among other things, he:

- criticized the fake news media, but not the entire press, and called for sources to be named and the media to be honest and fair
- repeated that the core conviction of the Movement is to put American citizens first.
- said the country has traded jobs to other nations for too long and defended other nations' borders while leaving their own wide open

- promised that the wall would be built, and soon, way ahead of schedule
- said the border would be secure, and bad people would be kept out, and continue to be removed from the country
- will stop the flood of drugs pouring into our country
- promised to rebuild our crumbling infrastructure
- pointed out that Obamacare is a failed healthcare law that doesn't work, and it covers very few people, but it would be repealed and replaced to make it much better and less expensive
- will address the national debt that has doubled in eight years
- will repair the disaster our foreign policy has become
- will act to deliver on the promise to Make America Great Again
- will use tax dollars not being spent on illegal immigration to rebuild American communities, and immigration officers are removing gang members, drug dealers, and criminal aliens from the country
- will work to reduce violent crime and support law enforcement
- will negotiate one-on-one trade deals, especially in Trans-Pacific region, terminating deals if necessary
- act to allow the Keystone and Dakota Access pipelines to be constructed using American-made pipes to create jobs
- work to promote American energy, including shale oil, natural gas, and clean coal, to put miners back to work, and regulations will be reduced to make the economy and job market more competitive
- will enact tax reform to again lower taxes on the middle class, American businesses, and simplify the tax code

- will encourage American corporations to make major investments in the US, expanding production, and hiring more workers
- will substantially upgrade all aspects of the military, making it stronger than ever before, to promote peace through strength
- will direct the defense community to develop a plan to eradicate ISIS
- repeated that national security begins with border security, which prevents foreign terrorists from entering the US
- promised to reduce taxes, cut regulations, support police, defend the flag, rebuild military, and take care of veterans, fulfilling promises made to the people of the United States
- stated that global cooperation is important, but America comes first and there is one allegiance that unites all citizens: America
- thanked the evangelical and Christian communities, communities of faith, rabbis, priests, and pastors for their record support for him.
- stated he believes that with faith in each other and in God, there is no goal too big or task too great for Americans to achieve.
- closed by saying the future belongs to all Americans and America is coming back stronger than ever before.

There is no question that Donald J. Trump intends to continue to work for America and the American People in his second term as President. With his website, Truth Social and Rumble platforms, the President continues to share his vision and plans for this nation. Now, it only remains to assure his election to the office in 2024.

SEVEN

Moving Beyond Maga

"...whenever any Form of Government becomes destructive of these ends, it is the Right of the People to alter or to abolish it, and to institute new Government, laying its foundation on such principles and organizing its powers in such form, as to them shall seem most likely to effect their Safety and Happiness"—from the Declaration of Independence

PRESIDENT TRUMP'S return to the Oval Office in 2025 will see him continue his America First agenda, with opposition from the Deep State, the Uniparty, and the Left. To Drain the Swamp, President Trump will need to deconstruct the Administrative State, which he was unable to do in his first term. His reclassification of federal employees under his Schedule F Executive Order will allow future presidents to curb the power of the Bureaucratic-Administrative State (BAS). Schedule F is a critical first step in restoring the Republic and must be codified into law by Congress. The Department of Justice and FBI must also be reformed or replaced to eliminate corruption and bias, and those who have violated their oaths *and the public's trust must be held accountable for their crimes and malfeasances. Budgetary restraint, energy independence, foreign policy that avoids foreign entanglements, and open-handed fair-trade policies must also be addressed. Structural changes including term limits, spending cuts, and restrictions on lobbyists and special interests, to break the corruption cycle and restore accountability to the People, cannot be neglected. Perhaps most importantly, MAGA Patriots must seek election at every level and to begin reclaiming the culture, especially Academia. The work of saving America is just beginning, and MAGA Patriots must put ordinary Americans first and agree to preserve and protect the system designed by the Founders to endure.*

WE KNOW what President Trump intends to do when he returns to the Oval Office in 2025. He will continue to pursue an America First agenda, and we can reasonably assume that the forces that have worked against him since 2015 will continue to do the same going forward. The Deep State, the Uniparty, the rabid Left all know that the rise of MAGA threatens their very existence. Therefore, MAGA Patriots must be prepared to face their opposition and support President Trump as he again tries to Drain the Swamp[1] and expose the Deep State, because only then can the work of restoring the Republic go forward.

During his first term, President Trump was able to make great strides in the first two of the three verticals[2]—national security and sovereignty/economic nationalism—but was stymied in his attempts to "Drain the Swamp" by deconstructing the Administrative State.

At numerous events, President Trump has spoken about moving rapidly to restore his "Schedule F" Executive Order[3] reclassifying some 50,000 federal employees and making them essentially at-will employees. Schedule F will allow the next and all future Presidents to greatly reign in the Bureaucratic-Administrative State (BAS).

These unelected, largely unaccountable denizens of the BAS have significant effects on policy that carry across administrations. They are basically decoupled from the effects of any elections, which is one of the main reasons why nothing much changes regardless of which party has "control" at the moment.

Every President must make some 4,000 appointments upon taking office, but these 50,000 apparatchiks of the BAS far outnumber the 4,000 "new blood" agents of an incoming President. They pass unchanged from administration to administration and largely account for the inertia that makes any one President's term much like any other. They enjoy employment protections that make firing them all but impossible (barring getting caught red-handed with a dead sex worker, a live goat, a half-empty jar of marmalade, and a weed whacker still running). By changing their status, any of them who actively resist a President's agenda can be pink-slipped—just like millions of recalcitrant, unproductive employees in the real world.

Elections come and go, but the BAS is eternal—at least until Schedule F is implemented!

Changing the status of thousands of bureaucrats with the President's Schedule F Executive Order is perhaps the single most important step the next President (hopefully, Trump 2.0) and a MAGA-controlled Congress can take to start unwinding the BAS. Without it, the Swamp will never be drained, the March of Progressivism cannot be halted, and the Deep State will never be more than temporarily inconvenienced.

It is telling that Biden's handlers wasted precious little time (2 days) before putting the repeal of President Trump's Schedule F Executive Order in front of Brandon for his signature.[4]

This Executive Order, like other pro-America First, pro-MAGA Executive Orders, should be codified by Congress as soon as possible. As we've seen, what one President can do with a stroke of the pen another can undo[5] just as easily. Having Congress pass laws duplicating the effects of critical Executive Orders gives another layer of protection to these actions.

President Trump's statements that he intends to move on this issue quickly when re-elected is one of the primary reasons the Powers That Be are working so frantically to keep Trump from being allowed to run again. When they are (hopefully) unsuccessful, it will turbocharge their efforts to "fortify"—what a normal person would call "rig" or "steal"—the 2024 election just as they did in 2020. We know that individuals in the Department of Justice and FBI colluded against Trump's campaigns in 2016, and 2020.[6] Why should we believe that 2024 will be any different?

As essential as Schedule F is to Draining the Swamp, it alone won't be enough. Dismantling the Deep State requires removing the corruption and politicization of multiple governmental agencies,[7] chief among them being the Department of Justice.

MAGA Patriots must fully support President Trump's efforts to reform and/or replace all or part of the Department of Justice,[8] especially the FBI.[9] We rely on justice to be blind, but our justice system gave up any pretense of impartiality and fairness—the very essence of being 'just'— years ago. This politicization[10] of what should be absolutely incorruptible must be stopped. Corruption and bias must be eliminated. Whether this can be done by mass-scale investigations and firings, or if it will require dissolving the FBI,[11] hosing out the DoJ stables and starting over from scratch is something that is beyond the scope of this small book.

We must trust President Trump and a cadre of loyal advisors (please God, let them be better than some of the ones he had the first time around!) to address the rehabilitation of the Department of Justice in a timely and comprehensive manner.

Lest you think this isn't needed, consider:

- Hunter Biden's laptop
- Jeffery Epstein's Island visitor and flight logs
- Hillary's email handling vs the FBI raid to seize Trump's documents at Mar-A-Lago
- Lois Lerner's complete lack of prosecution for her acts at the IRS
- Treatment of the "Peaceful Protestors" of Antifa and BLM vs the treatment of the Jan 6th "insurrectionists"

President Trump has promised to bring the Deep State to heel in his second term, and he has a record of keeping his promises. If he is successful in following through with Schedule F, it will be a major victory for the American people. Restoring confidence in the Department of Justice and the FBI will be another, equally major victory.

Once again, Congress must codify Schedule F into law as quickly as possible, despite the intense opposition to such a move that the Democrats, their allies, and the bureaucrats (and their unions) will bring to bear against it. There are very few hills worth dying on, but this is one of them. Schedule F is the key that unlocks the dams that maintain the Swamp. Without it, the Swamp will persist, and the

MAGA Movement will go the way of the Tea Party, the Whigs, and so many others.

Schedule F is a critical first step toward pruning the bloated administrative apparatus of the BAS briar patch. Cleaning up the DoJ is another necessary step. However, neither is sufficient in and of itself to complete the task.

To fully Drain the Swamp,[12] MAGA Leaders must be prepared to slaughter the occasional sacred cow, butcher bureaucracies, ravage regulations and regulators, lay into the lobbyists, and neuter the NGOs that have such a disproportionate influence on national policies (often, at taxpayer expense). Fortunately, it will be easy to determine the effectiveness of MAGA actions against the Swamp in real-time. Just listen to the volume of the screams....

As the Swamp begins to drain, the screams of the Swamp Critters will be horrible, loud, and unhinged. They'll pitch tantrum after tantrum every single time they don't get their way. As always, their Establishment RINO allies, their paid mobs, and their media bobbleheads will be right there with them. Condemnations and threats from both Left and RINO Right will fly thick and fast, but they must be ignored, slapped down, or laughed at. To make this possible, MAGA Patriots must be willing to support their MAGA Leaders against the resistance from the Establishment and their cronies, both Left and RINO Right.

Laughing at the Left and the RINOs will always be an effective tactic against them, even though (or perhaps because) it provokes the most drastic responses. There is precedence for this—President Trump used to troll the Leftists on Twitter several times a day and they never handled it well. As they did before, the Left's severe overreactions will only expose more of their true natures to the public, to MAGA's benefit.

That it's fun to watch humorless Lefties completely lose it and start spewing Marxist, Wokist stream-of-consciousness garbage after seeing a few well-chosen words in a Trump post is merely an unintended benefit. It never gets old.

MAGA Patriots will need all the fun they can find in the next few years. It's past time we as a nation faced some hard facts: we are effectively maxed out on all of our credit cards, overdrawn at the bank, and barely a step ahead of the loan sharks. By any realistic measure or generally accepted accounting practice, America is overextended, overdrawn, and broke. Our government has made financial promises that may be impossible to keep, and in the past Congress after Congress has lacked the foresight and spine to make even a token effort to address the structural problems baked into the government's spending. Remember Simpson-Boles?[13] No? Don't feel bad—nobody else does, either.[14] When was the last time Congress actually did its job and passed a budget? Not these endless continuing resolutions (which function more like raising the limit on a credit card than anything else), but a real budget, much less one that was balanced.

The deficit is unimaginably high, spending is out of control, and Congress and multiple administrations have kicked the budgetary can down the road for decades. Now, we've run out of road. The next kick may be the one that sends that can into the ditch. The budget and spending cuts that must—repeat, MUST—be made in the very near future will be painful, and completely beyond the capacity of the current crop of Congresspersons to enact. It will fall to newly-elected MAGA leaders to make these cuts and make them stick—despite the screams.

No one wants to be the one who shuts down the party by 'taking away the punchbowl', but it has to happen. The next administration will have to deal not only with decades of financial profligacy but also with Joe Biden and the Democrat's recent spending sprees. This will be painful under the best of circumstances, but it will be excruciating if it has to be done under the conditions of the Biden economy circa mid-2022. Our only hope for restoring some degree of sanity and solvency to the government lies in a return to a rapidly growing economy—like the one we enjoyed during the first two years under President Trump's America First policies.

The inevitable screams (sooooo many screams![15]) and overreactions to cutting back bloated government spending are the Left's go-to tactics when forced to defend the indefensible. Making the Lefties justify inane, outdated, or frankly counterproductive programs plays right into MAGA's hands. MAGA leaders can open more eyes to the absurdity of their policies and positions simply by asking Progressive Democrats to explain just how much "bang for the buck", in terms of actual benefit, the country gets for every dollar spent. Of course, they will have no answers based on facts, just feelings—just like always—and more people are realizing this every day.

Biden's policies are making this painfully obvious to everyone outside the Beltway: America can no longer afford to waste time and treasure on programs that simply do not work well (or at all) just because they provide positive feelings for the Elites.[16]

The next MAGA Congress will have to remind people that no matter how much it hurts now, it will be much, much worse if the entire economy, the dollar, and the monetary system collapse under the weight of too much government spending, for too long, for too many unnecessary things. I don't envy those Representatives and Senators who have to give that little speech.

During his first term, President Trump did not focus on budgetary restraint. Given everything else that he accomplished despite significant opposition, this is perhaps understandable. Also, the marked growth in the economy during Trump's first two years would have laid the groundwork for successfully tackling the structural problems in the federal budget later on, had circumstances turned out differently.

A return to the economic nationalism of the early Trump administration is vital to our nation's continued economic survival, much less our prosperity. The single most important factor in revitalizing the economy quickly is energy policy.

Energy is everything.[17] President Trump knows this, as his record shows.

The nation can expect a second Trump administration to return to the policies which made America energy independent in 2019. The incredible difference between President Trump's years in office—when domestic energy production was prioritized—and the disaster that has been the first years of the Biden Regime's anti-oil, anti-gas, anti-coal Green Raw Deal, Climate Scam agenda[18] could not be more striking.[19]

Nothing will have as drastic and positive an effect on the economy as turning America's energy production back up to full throttle. Gasoline and diesel prices will drop, which will bring down food and goods prices as the cost to both produce and transport them goes down. Supply chain woes will ease as transportation becomes cheaper. As energy supplies truly increase[20] (without the short-sighted, national security-threatening draining of the Strategic Petroleum Reserve), prices will naturally fall, reducing the cost to make and move goods and provide services. #Bidenflation at the pump and in the grocery store will wither more quickly under the return of Trumpian energy policy than any fiddling by the Federal Reserve can hope to arrange.

Pipelines and refineries will be built. Oil and gas leases on federal lands will once again be issued,[21] without the bureaucratic foot-dragging and double-speak that has become the standard passive-aggressive approach of the Biden administration. Clean coal will come back into fashion,[22] and our elderly, our young, and our vulnerable will have the heating and cooling they need without fear of solar- and wind-insufficiency power outages.[23]

The trees won't mind.[24] In fact, they'll continue to be quite happy with it.[25] As an added benefit, we won't be begging our frenemies and adversaries for oil, and we'll be able to export more crucial fossil fuels to our allies in Europe. After how badly Europe has suffered recently from a shortage of energy, I'm reasonably sure they'll appreciate it.

Renewable energy sources have their place,[26] but they will never reach the levels of output the American economy needs to sustain itself, much less grow. There are good arguments that 'easy' fossil fuels are rapidly being depleted,[27] which is why I am hopeful that the next administration will aggressively adopt an "all of the above, and what else can we bring online?" energy policy. New technologies and advances in batteries[28] and nuclear sources,[29] just to name two, offer the potential to substantially reduce our reliance on fossil fuels. But, like with solar and wind, at this time they lack the capacity to meet our needs.

The Green New Deal and other maladies of the Climate Scam[30] farce must be eliminated once and for all. While returning to our fossil fuel production levels of just a few years ago relieves the inflationary and supply-chain pressures of Bidenomics, we can move forward to aggressively develop practical, workable alternative energy sources like molten salt reactors and fusion[31] power plants, as well as new battery technologies[32] that remove our dependence on China and its Communist Party for lithium and other rare earth elements. China[33] and India[34] are both actively pursuing thorium-based reactor technologies. Despite American scientists having run the first successful molten salt reactor at Oak Ridge, Tennessee in 1965,[35] we lag significantly behind in this area. This technology has the potential to "burn" spent nuclear fuel from conventional water-cooled reactors (and old nuclear weapons),[36] but our own Nuclear Regulatory Committee has been a major stumbling block to advancing this potentially game-changing clean technology. Thankfully, these regulatory barriers began to improve under President Trump's leadership,[37] and may soon bear fruit.

The next administration can make developing innovative nuclear[38] and other technologies[39] a priority that will have significant long-term benefits for the economy, our standard of living, and our future energy security.

The Left knows their energy policies have failed[40] and angered the American people. They also know that seeing the difference between Trump—Biden—Trump again will kill any regard for their insane Green Raw Deal[41] energy policies for decades to come, for anyone with half a brain.

Naturally, the Left's base, having considerably less than half a normal brain's worth of intellect, will be largely unaffected.

The President pointed this out at Mar-A-Lago, when he talked about how the "pause" between his first and upcoming second term had a small silver lining: it has made the contrast between Trump policies and the Biden regime so glaringly obvious that no honest person can deny it.

Shortly after the 2025 inauguration, it will be time to begin investigating and harrying the Left and their RINO allies with exactly the same fervor and intensity they have applied to the President and his supporters—but unlike the Lefties, MAGA Leaders will have no need to fabricate, collude, cover up or create narratives[42] to justify their actions. It will be enough to rigorously, honestly, and transparently address the Left's crimes and malfeasances before bringing them to trial to face justice.

The Left has shown itself to be a master of Lawfare, weaponizing the apparatus of the legal system against President Trump and his supporters these last few years. They are long overdue for a taste of their own medicine. Again, unlike the Democrats and Never-Trump RINOs, MAGA Patriots won't have to bring in a producer[43] to stage show trials, kangaroo courts, kabuki theater hearings, or sham impeachments. Merely applying existing laws fairly and equitably to the guilty will be more than enough to administer that medicine. Justice can be delivered (although perhaps not in any court in the District of Columbia, rife with Democrats as it is) with a side of "sauce for the goose".

This cannot be avoided if there is to be any deterrence of similar acts in the future. In purely behavioralist terms, without an adverse consequence being applied to an undesired behavior, there is no motivation to change that behavior. Those who used their positions of authority to profit unfairly must be brought to justice. Those who perverted the system for their own political or personal gains should be reprimanded. All those who committed malfeasance under Color of Law[44] should suffer the full weight[45] of the law. Finally, those who committed election fraud must be punished. We must restore faith in our system—in our elections, in our institutions, and in our leaders—for our Republic to be fully restored.

There are numerous other changes that can and should be made to unwind many years of accumulated dross and corruption. Some would call this a "wish list". I prefer to call it "fixing what's broken". Listing all of what needs to be repaired, adjusted, or simply eliminated in the government[46] would take volumes, but here are just a few to spark your thinking.

Appointing more constitutional conservative judges who will interpret, rather than make, the law becomes possible with both the White House and Congress in MAGA hands. As recent decisions by the Supreme Court of the United States (SCOTUS) have reminded us, judicial appointments can have lasting impacts far beyond the term of office of the Presidents who appointed them. A MAGA-friendly Senate will also aid in this by rapidly providing their "advice and consent" to conservative judges.

Since most State and local judges are elected rather than appointed, local MAGA groups should also actively work to elect solid constitutionally conservative judges. Former Speaker Tip O'Neill said, "All politics is local," and he was absolutely correct. Having MAGA judges up and down the judicial hierarchy will be a useful tool to block the machinations of the Left. The Left has enjoyed decades of using the courts to achieve their ends, especially those too radical to ever hope to pass a State Legislature or Congress. It's time for conservatives to enjoy the same advantage in the judiciary.

One incredible aspect of President Trump's four years in office is that he is the first President in decades who did NOT start a war. No new wars on Trump's watch—not one! Of course, this didn't endear him to the military-industrial complex (Ike was right!) or the Neo-Conservative (neo-clowns that they are) hawks in the War Party, but as a Presidential accomplishment it is remarkable. His efforts to broker peace deals[47] in the Middle East were as impressive[48] as his successful trade deals, and we can only pray that he continues to enjoy both diplomatic and trade successes during his second term.

In many ways, President Trump's first term combined key elements of Washington's Farewell Address and Jefferson's first Inaugural Address. He avoided any (unnecessary) foreign entanglements but also worked to create new alliances and pacts[49] to benefit America and the nations in those alliances. President Trump extended the hand of fair trade but fought against the unfair "free" trade practices and pacts that previous administrations had inflicted on this nation and its People.

Finally, President Trump worked diligently to Build The Wall. The opposition from within his own party was as severe as any from the opposition, and a full border Wall remains unfinished. Now Joe Biden's policies have caused our southern border to collapse, with tens of thousands of invaders flooding into our nation every month. This must stop, and with a MAGA Congress supporting him, President Donald J. Trump will stop it.

Our immigration system was broken before Biden took office. Now it's been absolutely destroyed.[50] The American people are ready for it to be fixed--not with a bandage or good intentions but actually fixed.[51] Securing the border is a necessary first step in doing this because so long as the border is a sieve every other immigration issue is meaningless. Every option[52] must be on the table, including the repeal of Teddy Kennedy's 1965 Immigration Act, the 1990 Immigration Act, and possibly all six mini-amnesties that passed Congress in the 1990s.[53] Congress should also strongly consider revisiting Barbara Jordan's 1996 blue-ribbon commission on immigration and its recommendations.[54]

As with the budget[55] literally decades of fumbling have brought us to the point where hard, painful decisions must be made on immigration policy. A Congress which seeks, first and foremost, to make the world safe for re-election[56] will never make these hard choices. They haven't yet, so why start now?

The need for term limits[57] is all too clear. Term limits for Congress will be fought tooth and nail by legacy members of both parties, but this is a critical first step[58] in restoring accountability[59] to the elected leaders of the People. Congress was never meant to be a life sentence, but that is what it has become. With term limits, Representatives and Senators will know that their tenure in the halls of power is finite and that at some point they will have to return to being ordinary citizens, just like the rest of us. This could be the seed from which a sense of national responsibility grows, and may make some long-overdue immigration changes, budgetary sense, discipline over reckless, out-of-control spending, and general sanity take root.

Inevitably, special interests and their armies of lobbyists will do everything in their power to preserve the status quo. Blocking the influence of K Street, if not reigning it in, is both a near- and long-term goal every MAGA Patriot must embrace. The lobbyists and the huge amounts of money they command are an integral part of the Swamp, and need draining as much as any other part of it.[60]

The Left loathes that Donald Trump succeeded despite #TheResistance, RussiaRussiaRussia, a Twitter ban, and everything else they could throw at him. The Establishment Right despises Trump for actually doing what the people elected him to do, without caring too much about their feelings, rituals, and sense of "how things are done". America's enemies abroad both fear and respect him, and our Enemies Domestic hate him because he's winning, they're losing,[61] and President Trump and MAGA Patriots are laughing at them.

It's ironic that the 1960's radicals that were Alinsky's target audience for his Rules have become The Establishment, while America First, MAGA Patriots are called radicals (and worse) today. It's even more ironic that wanting to restore the nation, address the crimes committed in the 2020 election and return to the Constitution is considered a radical idea—but these are the "interesting"[62] times in which we live.[63]

MAGA has made the transition from campaign slogan to Movement and is in the process of becoming something much, much more. It has the potential to form the basis of a new political philosophy that's not really new at all. If it can continue to grow, create that new/old ideology and transcend the politics of the moment, it can be successful at restoring a Republic that has lost its way.

Moving beyond MAGA the campaign slogan and into the era of MAGA the political philosophy, MAGA Patriots and supporters of America First policies will:

- Accept that restoring the Constitutional Republic envisioned by the Founders will be a long-term struggle, and prepare ourselves accordingly—mentally, physically, fiscally, and spiritually
- Restore confidence in our elections and the election process, including addressing the stolen Presidential election of 2020
- Diligently work to take control of Congress and the White House through the election of strong MAGA leaders—especially Donald J. Trump in 2024—realizing that this will be an ongoing process in every election cycle
- Return to an America First policy at home and abroad, beginning with national and economic security, and including energy security

- Restore America's energy independence as quickly as possible, by expanding all forms of energy production
- Return to a foreign policy that seeks to avoid foreign entanglements instead of pursuing nation-building and interference in other nation's affairs in the guise of expanding the American empire
- Pursue an open-handed fair trade policy with any nation who will trade fairly with us, while avoiding the trap of free, unfair trade agreements
- Resist globalism wherever it may be encountered, and as we support America First, support other nation's right to do the same for themselves
- Offer the open hand of friendship to all, but never fear to be strong, swift, and sure when American force is necessary to protect American citizens and legitimate American interests
- Never forget that American citizenship is a privilege and a gift, and never allow it to be stolen or bestow its benefits upon those who are unworthy or undeserving
- Drain the Swamp, starting with the President's Schedule F Executive Order, then having Congress codify that EO immediately as a first step towards reigning in the regulatory state. We must rescue businesses and individuals from crushing overregulation for our economy to grow and the people to prosper
- Begin restoring our judiciary to its interpretive, non-activist roots by appointment to the bench of MAGA judges, and by electing MAGA judges at the State and local levels.
- Work for structural changes, beginning with term limits, budgetary restraint and restrictions on lobbyists and special interests, to break up the Congressional Uniparty

corruption cycle and restore accountability to their constituents by our representatives
- Encourage MAGA Patriots to seek election at every level, from the School Board and City Council to the State House, Governor's Office and everything in between. Eliminating Progressivism, Wokism and the other corrosive ideologies of the Left in our local schools, communities, and States is just as important (if not more so) than eliminating them in Washington.
- Begin reclaiming Academia, first at the local level through the school boards, and then higher education as our MAGA-educated kids enter those institutions, knowing these efforts will take at least a decade to begin bearing fruit

These are by no means all the things that must be done, but hopefully are a good starting point. The work of Restoring the Republic will be done at all levels, from the smallest hamlets to the marble halls of the Nation's Capital. Each needs the full support of the others. Federal, State, and Local; all are important and necessary for the MAGA Movement to succeed.

Remember the four basic MAGA questions. Use them as both guideposts and barriers as the Movement grows, especially the first, most important one:

> *Does it (whatever 'it' may be) promote, protect, defend and/or advance the cause of ordinary Americans?*

MAGA Patriots will often disagree about some issues, or on their particulars. So long as they put ordinary Americans first and agree that the system designed by the Founders should be preserved and protected, the MAGA Movement will endure.

The work of saving America—of putting America First, Making it Great Again, and then Keeping it Great for our children and grandchildren—is just beginning.

May God bless these United States and all their People.

EIGHT

Bonus Chapter—The Sins Of Trump And The Big Steal

"We are fast approaching the stage of the ultimate inversion: the stage where the government is free to do anything it pleases, while the citizens may act only by permission; which is the stage of the darkest periods of human history, the stage of rule by brute force."—Ayn Rand

MILLIONS OF MAGA PATRIOTS support the ideals of the Founders, including limited, honest, transparent government that protects individual rights and liberties. These Patriots stand against America's enemies and support President Donald J. Trump. Trump's America First policies produced explosive economic growth and prosperity, and no new foreign wars, in his first term. However, Trump and his policies threatened the administrative state, the Deep State, and the globalist elites seeking the Great Reset, which is why the 2020 election was stolen. During Galileo's trial for heresy, he invited his inquisitors to look through his telescope, but they refused to see the evidence of his claims, covering one eye so they could truthfully say "I see no evidence". Similarly, too many Americans *have been One-eyed Cardinals, refusing to acknowledge the evidence of rampant fraud in the 2020 election. MAGA must insist that the stolen election be acknowledged and those responsible be held accountable, as a first step towards insuring honest elections in the future. The MAGA Movement must stand up for America First, the Constitution, and the People, and grow to influence all levels of government. MAGA is more than a campaign slogan. It represents the hopes, dreams, and aspirations of millions here in America and around the world.*

MILLIONS OF MAGA PATRIOTS support the ideals of the Founders —a limited, honest, transparent government that protects individual rights and liberties instead of trampling them.

These Patriots stand against the enemies of America both foreign and domestic. They stand with their fellow Patriots against the enemies of the MAGA Movement, within and without. They stand with President Donald J. Trump, the founder and leader of the MAGA Movement.

President Trump's America First policies worked before, and will again. The evidence of his first two years in office is undeniable. Explosive economic growth and prosperity, a shrinking wealth gap between rich and poor, no new foreign wars, and so much more— President Trump showed everyone that putting America and her people first produced miraculous results. Despite constant attacks from every quarter, Donald J. Trump did what his detractors said was impossible, time and time again. And then, when a once-in-a-century global pandemic struck, a newly-revived and energized American economy was there to meet the challenge.

Trump's success, and the possibility that he would continue to succeed as the pandemic waned, was why the will of the American people was thwarted by the 2020 election.

Trump and his MAGA policies threatened the permanent bureaucracy, the administrative state that for years has dominated the DC Swamp. He threatened the globe-spanning machinations of the Deep State[1] and the cozy NGO-Lobbyist-Uniparty status quo of relationships inside the Washington Beltway,

Donald J. Trump and the America First, MAGA agenda he championed threatened the decades-long march of progressivism and globalism of the "liberal world order". The first Trump administration threatened to expose the Deep State, drain the DC Swamp, and disrupt the Great Reset so fervently desired by the globalist elites.

This was Trump's penultimate sin and heresy. A United States of America, freed from the clutches of the globalists, seeking first and foremost the welfare of the American people, could not be allowed to arise in the 21st century. Trump had to be brought down, his vision thwarted, his supporters maligned and broken, and his repairing of America's sovereignty stopped.

When Galileo was being tried for heresy, it's said he took his Inquisitors, including several Cardinals, to his home. He showed them his telescope and invited them to look for themselves, to see that his observations about the Earth and planets circling the Sun were correct. As the story goes, each Cardinal covered his eye with his hand as he looked through the telescope. Each Cardinal could then legitimately say "I see no evidence".

Since November 2020, we've seen too many One-Eyed Cardinals who see "no evidence".

"Eppur si muove" (And yet, it moves) was what Galileo allegedly said following his conviction for heresy and forced recantation. Eventually, of course, he would be vindicated. Science and history would prove him correct, and several hundred years later, in 1992, the Catholic Church formally admitted that Galileo was right all along.

Eppur si muove. And yet, it moves.

How many times have we been told there is "no evidence" of rampant fraud, chicanery, and dirty trickery in the 2020 election? Despite the incessant repetition of the "no evidence" narrative, "And yet, it was stolen" is a truth many Americans accept about the 2020 election.[2] Every day, more Americans realize this, thanks to the work of stalwarts like Mike Lindell, Dinesh D'Souza, and many others. The evidence of rampant fraud was there to be seen within hours or days,[3] and despite the efforts of corrupt, fraudulent officials in multiple states, it continues to accumulate.

The stolen election of 2020 must be acknowledged, and those responsible must be held accountable for their actions. This is the first, crucial step the MAGA Movement must take if it is to survive.

It may not be possible to undo the results of the stolen election of 2020 (although I am unwilling to abandon that as a possibility), but it must be openly admitted, and the perpetrators of the fraud at every level brought to justice.

In Philadelphia in 1776, there was no method for the Colonies to separate themselves from the British Empire. They did it anyway. They made a method and made it work. They had exhausted every other option available to them and felt they had no choice. They were brave men, determined to live free--qualities we sadly seem to be lacking in many of our leaders at this point.

If there is a litmus test for the MAGA Movement, it should be this one question: was the 2020 election stolen, denying Donald J. Trump re-election to a second term as President of the United States?

There is only one acceptable answer to this question.

Yes.

Putting aside possible remedies for the 2020 debacle, it is imperative that such a heinous act never be allowed to happen again—ever. We must have honest elections that reflect the will of the People (i.e., eligible, legal voters). We must be confident in our election results, and the process must be transparent and open with the final numbers verified by multiple means.

There must be accountability at every step of the election process, and that must begin with clean, accurate voter rolls. We must have secure (hard copy) ballots and a verification process that ensures that only legal ballots cast by legal voters within the legal timeframe of the election are counted. Finally, there must be a reliable, accurate, verifiable counting process with built-in safeguards and auditing procedures that provides accurate tallies of the legitimate votes cast.

As I've said, this is not impossible. It is, however, absolutely necessary if the Republic is to survive. Without honest elections, we are at best an Oligarchy, and at worst a Banana Republic-esque dictatorship.

We've had over two years of that already, and the consequences have been disastrous. Those who gathered at the Capitol to protest in what was honestly a "mostly peaceful" fashion (without any significant burning, looting, or rioting) have been accused of being insurrectionists, and some of them have been incarcerated in America's very own gulag. Meanwhile, allies of the true insurrectionists—those who orchestrated the stolen election—have attempted to skew the public's perception of the events of January 6th with a series of carefully orchestrated "hearings" (aka "witch hunts"), complete with biased witnesses, predetermined conclusions and professionally-produced and directed multimedia presentations. Unfortunately for them, their little dog & pony show accomplished little more than showcasing their own venality, and some of them have already had an electoral reckoning, with more sure to come.

Eppur si muove.

Some have suggested that the MAGA Movement should replace Donald Trump as standard-bearer and leader. These people have openly discussed "Trumpism without Trump", to carry the MAGA banner forward "without the baggage" of the founder of the Movement. Oddly enough, it seems that the people supporting this initiative are the ones who would be carrying that MAGA banner...but I'm sure that's purely a coincidence.[4]

While passing the torch from President Trump to MAGA's next leader(s) is inevitable at some point, now is NOT the time. With the 2024 election already looming, cooperating with the MAGA Movement's most rabid enemies to unseat President Trump is highly fraught, verging on asinine. Of course, circumstances may change between now and then, but right now only Donald John Trump has the resources and support to carry MAGA forward successfully.

The MAGA Movement will need successors to the President, and I'm pleased to see so many great leaders rising up to formally join the MAGA Movement. However, MAGA is about more than just the White House—MAGA must stretch from School Boards and City Councils, through Statehouses and Capitals, through Congress to the Oval Office, and then indirectly, through appointment and confirmation, to the Supreme Court of these United States. We can not, will not, must not settle for anything less.

We are in the midst of a reawakening of the American spirit, and America's enemies are rightfully terrified of what they face. It is time for the MAGA Movement to grow up, clench up and stand up for America First and Foremost, her ideals, her Constitution, and her People. As a group of those first Americans said years ago:

> "...with a firm reliance on the protection of divine Providence, we mutually pledge to each other our Lives, our Fortunes and our sacred Honor."

MAGA is already so much more than a campaign slogan. It represents the hopes, dreams, and aspirations of millions of people, not only here in America but around the world. It has become an Ideal to which a People can aspire.

A man can be imprisoned. A man can be banished. A man can be killed. An Ideal can never be chained, vanished, or destroyed. Truth can be suppressed, but always remains true.

Eppur si muove.

NINE

Afterward—The Red Speech

"If you want to know what your enemy will do next, listen to what he says."--Sun Tzu

ON SEPTEMBER 1ST, 2022, Joe Biden's Red Speech changed everything and nothing at the same time. It changed nothing because the all-out war between the radical, Progressive Left and conservative, populist MAGA Right has been ongoing since Trump's campaign in 2015. However, it changed everything because it was so blatant and un-Presidential that Americans from across the political spectrum had their eyes forced open. Biden called his political opponents "threats to democracy," with no compromise or coming together being possible. The Red Speech made it clear that Biden's handlers and his base see only victory or defeat against the MAGA Movement, and MAGA has no choice but to pick up the gauntlet. The MAGA Movement will pursue its goals within the framework of the law, and the first step is to have honest, fair, and transparent elections with verified election integrity. MAGA must elect MAGA candidates at every level and hold them accountable for their *actions. With strong MAGA leaders in place, the true work of restoring the Republic can begin. The stakes are high, and the MAGA Movement is determined to fight for them.*

Working on this book in late August of 2022, I saw ample reason to despair, along with a few rays of hope. Then, on the night of September 1st, Joe Biden was led from Independence Hall and placed behind a podium. He read what came up on the teleprompter,[1] and all but declared war on more than 70 million Americans.

The Red Speech[2] changed everything and nothing at the same time.

It changed nothing in that the all-out war between radical, Progressive Left and conservative, populist MAGA Right has been going on since the early days of Trump's campaign in 2015. Most of those involved on both sides know it, accept it, and plan accordingly.

The Red Speech changed everything because it was so blatant, so over-the-top, and so un-Presidential that Americans from all across the political spectrum had their eyes forced open. The Left calls MAGA Nazis and fascists, but here was a President giving a speech in a setting straight out of Nuremberg. Biden called his political opponents "threats to democracy", with not a single word given to compromise or coming together. How can you claim to be President of all Americans when everyone who voted for your opponent is a "threat to the soul of democracy"?

Biden's next-day backpedaling notwithstanding, the Red Speech made it perfectly clear that Biden's handlers (and most of his base) see only victory or defeat against the MAGA Movement.

So be it. Their puppet Biden threw down the gauntlet. The MAGA Movement has no choice but to pick it up.

No one sane chooses bloody revolution as a first, second, or third option. The MAGA Movement should, and will, do everything possible within the framework of the law to pursue our goals.

First and foremost, we as a nation must have honest, fair, and transparent elections—and we should be confident that is the case. This requires that we develop systems to assure election integrity, not just accept assurances that our elections are secure. Millions of us have lost trust in our elections and those who are responsible for them, so we must verify every election, every time, without exception. This is the cost of destroying our trust in our elections, and we as a nation must now pay that cost going forward.

The MAGA Movement must elect MAGA candidates at every level, then hold them accountable for their actions. Those who fail to deliver on their MAGA promises will have to be replaced, and this cycle will have to be repeated every election to keep MAGA ideas and values from being circumvented or ignored.

Then, with strong MAGA leaders in place, the true work of restoring the Republic can begin.

We know the stakes, and we know they are worth fighting for. May God bless America and the MAGA Movement.

TEN

A Note on References

Given the realities of modern publishing, especially e-book publishing, and the proliferation of e-book readers, traditional book references that include page number along with title and chapter are difficult, if not impossible to cite correctly.

The ability to increase or decrease font size, line spacing and margins for the convenience of individual readers has significant effects on the numbers of words on every page, making page numbers highly variable, if not completely useless.

This author values being able to increase the font size on his e-reader to accommodate his tired old eyes, which is why most of the books read during the preparation of this manuscript were read in their e-book formats.

Consequently, most book references are given only as chapters in a particular work. While this may inconvenience or irritate some, it is a necessary adjustment to these new-fangled times.

Similarly, Appendix 1 contains only the most basic information about books referenced in this work, including Author, Title, Publisher and Year of Publication. That should be more than enough for Amazon or Google to find it for you. If not, find a Librarian or Bookseller who was alive when Nixon resigned and throw yourself on their mercy.

ELEVEN

Appendix 1

Supplemental Reading List of highly recommended books cited in this work:

ANGELO M. CODEVILLA, ***The Ruling Class***, Beaufort Books, 2010

VICTOR DAVIS HANSON, ***The Case for Trump***, Basic Books, 2020

KURT SCHLICHTER, ***Conservative Insurgency***, Post Hill Press, 2014

DONALD J TRUMP, ***Great Again***, Threshold Editions; Reprint edition, 2015

. . .

CHARLIE KIRK, *The MAGA Doctrine*, Broadside/HarperCollins, 2020

LOU DOBBS, *The Trump Century*, Broadside/HarperCollins, 2020

MICHAEL FRANZESE, *Mafia Government*, Lioncrest Publishing, 2022

PETER NAVARRO, *Taking Back Trump's America*, Bombardier Books/Post Hill Press, 2022

VOX DAY, *SJWs Always Lie*, Castalia House, 2015

TUCKER CARLSON, *Ship of Fools*, Free Press, 2018

SEBASTIAN GORKA, *The War for America's Soul*, Regnery Publishing, 2019

MOLLY HEMINGWAY, *Rigged: How the Media, Big Tech and the Democrats Seized Our Elections*, Regnery Publishing, 2021

JOE HOFT, *The Steal I* and *The Steal II*, Independently Published, 2022

. . .

Patrick Colbeck, ***The 2020 Coup***, McHenry Press, 2022

Lawrence Sellin, ***Restoring the Republic,*** Independently Published, 2013

Thomas Sowell, ***The Vision of the Anointed***, Basic Books, 1996

TWELVE

Appendix 2
_____

Important Documents

DOCUMENTS THAT ARE critical to understanding the origins of the American Experiment, the Trump phenomenon and the MAGA Movement:

THE FOUNDING DOCUMENTS (Declaration of Independence, Constitution, Bill of Rights) are available at:

https://www.archives.gov/founding-docs

WASHINGTON'S FAREWELL Address

https://founders.archives.gov/documents/Washington/05-20-02-0440-0002

. . .

JEFFERSON'S FIRST Inaugural Address

https://jeffersonpapers.princeton.edu/selected-documents/first-inaugural-address-0

TRUMP'S 2015 Presidential Announcement

Video: https://www.youtube.com/watch?v=apjNfkysjbM

TRUMP'S 2016 Inaugural Address

Video: https://www.youtube.com/watch?v=a-mfhjaPvsM

TRUMP'S 2020 RNC Acceptance Speech

Transcript: https://www.theepochtimes.com/mkt_app/read-full-transcript-of-president-trumps-rnc-acceptance-speech_3479265.html

Video: https://www.youtube.com/watch?v=RhL9iFkBaus

TRUMP'S 2022 America First address

Transcript: https://www.rev.com/blog/transcripts/donald-trump-speaks-at-america-first-agenda-summit-in-washington-dc-transcript

Video: https://www.c-span.org/video/?521940-1/president-trump-speaks-america-policy-institute-summit

. . .

Appendix 2 • 123

Trump's 2022 CPAC Address

Transcript: https://www.rev.com/blog/transcripts/former-president-donald-trump-speaks-at-cpac-8-06-22-transcript

Video: https://www.youtube.com/watch?v=KJTlo4bQL5c&t=1378s

Trump's 2022 Mar-A-Lago Campaign Announcement

Transcript: https://www.rev.com/blog/transcripts/former-president-trump-announces-2024-presidential-bid-transcript

Video: https://www.youtube.com/watch?v=8tSYwJ1_htE

Trump 2023 CPAC Address

Transcript: https://www.rev.com/blog/transcripts/trump-speaks-at-cpac-2023-transcript

Video: https://rumble.com/v2binw8-live-president-donald-trump-delivers-remarks-at-cpac.html

The Red Speech

Transcript:

https://www.whitehouse.gov/briefing-room/speeches-remarks/2022/09/01/remarks-by-president-bidenon-the-continued-battle-for-the-soul-of-the-nation/

About the Author

Doc Contrarian doesn't (quite) remember JFK's assassination but does remember the first moon landing, Nixon going to China, Carter's "Malaise", Reagan's hot mic "the missiles are on their way", Bush I's "read my lips—no new taxes", Bill Clinton's "it depends what 'is' is", the fall of the Berlin Wall, Bush II's "Mission Accomplished", several of Obama's off-the-teleprompter moments, and a fair amount of recent history, too. So, he's old enough to know better and close enough to his expiration date to not care a whole lot.

He's been described as a Conservatarian Contrarian, and that's probably as good a label as any. He identifies as a Constitutional conservative, and his pronouns are Doctor/Doctor and Doctor. At least that's what they are this week. He makes no promises for the future.

As he is fond of saying, "Don't feel special. I trigger everybody." As a matter of policy and principle, he does NOT discriminate—he hates everyone equally, because it's the only way to be fair.

Follow Doc Contrarian **@DocContrarian** on Twitter, Gab, GETTR and Truth Social, and on Substack https://doccontrarian.substack.com

Correspondence regarding this book may be addressed to BeyondMAGA@protonmail.com.

Don't expect much, and be patient as you wait for a reply. He hates email almost as much as he does Uniparty scum, but usually checks it once a month or so, whether it needs it or not.

If you have to be told that Doc Contrarian is a *nom de plume*, he doesn't have a whole lot for you.

Copyright 2023 by Doc Contrarian

All rights reserved.

Cover Design by Doc Contrarian

Cover photograph by clipground.com

ISBN (paperback) 979-8391874874

ISBN (hardback) 979-8391884262

Published by Doc Contrarian

USA

Correspondence address: BeyondMAGA@protonmail.com

❀ Created with Vellum

Notes

Disclaimer and Essential Information

1. https://peternavarro.com/the-navarro-report/

Introduction

1. This is a bit of an oversimplification, but a full discussion of the psychodynamics involved has been omitted in the interest of brevity and readability.
2. https://www.philstockworld.com/2017/03/08/mccain-institutes-failure-to-use-donations-for-antitrafficking-purposes-raises-questions/
3. https://www.youtube.com/watch?v=m6JbemSdORo
4. https://thefederalist.com/2022/03/15/kamala-harris-quotes-as-motivational-posters-because-the-time-to-be-inspired-is-every-day/ and https://thefederalist.com/2022/07/13/kamala-harris-quotes-as-motivational-posters-part-2/
5. https://electrek.co/2022/07/25/average-electric-car-price-hit-66000-us-whole-story/
6. Attributed to Admiral Raphael Semmes, from his ***Memoirs of Service Afloat, During the War Between The States***. There is some argument as to whether or not this is apocryphal, for this discussion as well as other statements by Mr. Lincoln about his financial motivations regarding secession, see https://civilwartalk.com/threads/apocryphal-lincoln-quote.123191/
7. https://k12.hillsdale.edu/Curriculum/The-Hillsdale-1776-Curriculum/
8. https://www.theepochtimes.com/the-true-story-of-1619-and-americas-origins-op-ed_4230030.html
9. https://node-1.2000mules.com/
10. https://selectioncode.com/
11. https://momentoftruthsummit.com/?msclkid=57f38c84c0fb18c5d047efd5207f8d1f
12. The Destructionist Phase of American History https://link.theepochtimes.com/mkt_app/the-destructionist-phase-of-american-history_4671089.html
13. https://spectator.org/americas-ruling-class/

1. The Origins Of The Maga Movement

1. The War for America's Soul (pp. 31-32)
2. https://www.thebalancemoney.com/tarp-bailout-program-3305895
3. https://spectator.org/americas-ruling-class/
4. Codevilla, Angelo M.; Limbaugh, Rush. ***The Ruling Class***. Beaufort Books.
5. https://www.merriam-webster.com/words-at-play/words-were-watching-spox, shortened form of "spokesperson" or "spokesman"
6. Made in 1968
7. Reportedly, McCain's Admiral father suppressed the information about his son's behavior while a POW at the time, but it did come out later, in part because of other pilots with whom he shared captivity. He may, in fact have succumbed to torture, resulting in the name "Songbird": https://www.washingtonexaminer.com/news/retired-general-torture-worked-on-john-mccain-thats-why-they-call-him-songbird-john.

    For more on McCain's questionable history throughout his Senate career, see https://thewashingtonstandard.com/the-truth-is-that-john-songbird-mccain-was-a-traitor/
8. https://www.denverpost.com/2008/03/08/democrats-fear-brokered-convention/
9. https://www.latimes.com/la-oe-ehrenstein19mar19-story.html
10. https://www.newsmax.com/insidecover/obama-parody-la-times/2008/12/29/id/327342/
11. https://www.thetentacle.com/2021/03/joe-biden-50-years-of-lies-and-gaffes/
12. https://www.baltimoresun.com/opinion/op-ed/bs-ed-op-0913-joe-biden-gaffes-20200910-nfcd3z575rfn3cijxkzosa2k6y-story.html
13. https://thefreethoughtproject.com/government-corruption/clinton-cash-documentary-exposes
14. https://youtu.be/EgIFV7jXBFQ
15. https://www.cnn.com/2007/POLITICS/01/31/biden.obama/
16. https://www.latimes.com/la-oe-ehrenstein19mar19-story.html
17. https://www.bbc.com/news/world-europe-34277960
18. https://www.netadvisor.org/wp-content/uploads/2020/09/2010-03-16-Executing-U.S.-Health-Care-with-a-Self-Executing-Rule.pdf
19. https://www.netadvisor.org/2020/09/29/the-truth-about-obamacare/
20. For a concise summary of the scandals of the Obama administration, and how the stage was set for the perfidy of 2020, see Ch. 1 of Sebastian Gorka's ***The War For America's Soul***, specifically:

    "This was Obama's White House. From the targeting of American patriots at home via the IRS, to missile strikes killing Americans abroad without due process before the law, the Obama administration had no qualms—none—with using the incredible might of the federal government against those it did not like, or wanted to eliminate. That is how we arrive at the plot to subvert candidate Trump's

campaign through the use of the Department of Justice (DOJ), FBI, CIA, and National Security Agency (NSA), for political purposes."

21. https://nypost.com/2016/08/09/emails-reveal-hillarys-shocking-pay-for-play-scheme/
22. https://townhall.com/tipsheet/mattvespa/2016/12/30/huffpo-editor-with-the-democrats-in-ruins-you-have-to-ask-whether-obama-was-good-for-the-party-n2265325
23. https://a.co/4kYGJeT
24. https://www.thoughtco.com/anti-federalists-4129289
25. https://teachingamericanhistory.org/document/constitutional-government-in-the-united-states/, last accessed 8/24/2022
26. https://www.wsj.com/articles/BL-WB-42869

2. But Is It Maga?

1. https://justthenews.com/government/federal-agencies/fri-head-us-oil-and-gas-association-says-biden-admin-kneecapped
2. https://www.thethinkingconservative.com/extensive-list-of-trump-administration-accomplishments/
3. https://amgreatness.com/2022/09/22/a-natcon-coninc-mashup/
4. https://www.goodreads.com/quotes/837554-i-didn-t-leave-the-democratic-party-the-democratic-party-left
5. https://www.washingtontimes.com/news/2014/aug/14/piscopo-confessions-of-a-disillusioned-democrat/
6. https://www.idahocountyfreepress.com/opinion/letter-i-didn-t-leave-the-democratic-party-it-left-me/article_59826338-3119-11ec-994f-b35fe9c628a7.html
7. https://www.reddit.com/r/unpopularopinion/comments/8gai3u/i_didnt_leave_the_democratic_party_the_democratic/

3. Maga, The Tea Party, And The Gop

1. https://www.politico.com/magazine/story/2016/08/tea-party-pacs-ideas-death-214164
2. https://www.ammoland.com/2014/06/can-the-tea-party-take-over-the-gop/
3. https://www.theatlantic.com/politics/archive/2014/03/emperor-mitch-mcconnell-pledges-crush-tea-party-rebellion/358995/
4. https://reason.com/2018/02/11/the-tea-party-is-dead-long-live-liberty/
5. https://www.huffpost.com/entry/trump-liz-cheney-impeach_n_62fd00f4e4b071ea958bcb3f
6. https://www.youtube.com/watch?v=5KTOPuCfSTE, 5:20
7. https://www.youtube.com/watch?v=nt7-WKXL5vw
8. https://www.thegatewaypundit.com/2022/11/big-day-trump-endorsed-candidates-

132 • Notes

fake-news-media-will-not-report-9-losses-174-wins-far/
9. https://thepoliticalinsider.com/maga-rep-matt-gaetz-torches-mcfailures-mcconnell-and-mccarthy-for-midterm-results/
10. https://truthsocial.com/users/DC_Draino/statuses/109314566683405935

4. Maga Enemies

1. https://time.com/5936036/secret-2020-election-campaign/
2. https://www.independentsentinel.com/hillary-clintons-obamanesque-vision-for-america/
3. https://www.westernjournal.com/poll-majority-likely-voters-now-believe-cheating-impacted-results-2020-election/
4. For more on how America's Elites have enriched themselves by aiding China's goals against America, I highly recommend Peter Schweizer's **Red-Handed: How American Elites Get Rich Helping China Win**, Harper, 2022.
5. https://www.globalsecurity.org/military/world/china/24-character.htm
6. https://f6p2k4m9.rocketcdn.me/wp-content/uploads/2022/08/IRS_Job_Posting-2.webp
7. https://libertyscholar.org/the-1619-project/
8. https://www.heritage.org/american-founders/commentary/the-real-goals-the-1619-project
9. https://www.usatoday.com/story/opinion/2020/11/01/donald-trump-african-american-black-economic-progress-vote-column/6081310002/
10. https://www.politico.com/news/2020/11/01/trump-black-americans-policies-433744
11. https://fee.org/articles/why-free-speech-on-campus-is-under-attack-blame-marcuse/
12. https://en.wikipedia.org/wiki/Fabian_Society
13. https://fee.org/articles/herbert-marcuse-the-philosopher-behind-the-ideology-of-the-anti-fascists/
14. https://www.gp.org/green_new_deal
15. https://www.theguardian.com/commentisfree/2012/feb/17/eugenics-skeleton-rattles-loudest-closet-left
16. https://www.theepochtimes.com/the-destructionist-phase-of-american-history_4671089.html
17. https://www.washingtonpost.com/opinions/2022/08/29/schedule-f-trump-civil-service-politics/
18. https://www.axios.com/2022/07/23/donald-trump-news-schedule-f-executive-order
19. https://www.breitbart.com/politics/2022/07/23/donald-trump-on-schedule-f-executive-order-to-drain-the-swamp-we-need-to-fire-the-swamp/
20. https://detv.us/2022/05/18/us-aid-to-ukraine-looks-like-a-money-laundering-scheme-rt-de/

21. https://integritas360.com/corruption-what-ngos-dont-want-you-to-know/
22. https://www.nap.edu/read/10240/chapter/20
23. https://www.huffpost.com/entry/the-neoclowns-are-at-it-a_b_27989
24. https://youtu.be/a-vHK3kO3wI
25. https://youtu.be/60MzTlrOCXQ
26. https://www.weforum.org/great-reset/
27. https://youtu.be/NcAO4-o_4Ug
28. https://www.louderwithcrowder.com/big-tech-censor-liberal
29. https://www.zerohedge.com/geopolitical/total-crockun-american-taibbi-exposes-censorious-arm-state-sponsored-blacklisting
30. https://www.washingtontimes.com/news/2022/apr/12/mark-zuckerbergs-donations-rigged-the-2020-electio/
31. https://www.zerohedge.com/political/facebook-fined-25m-washington-state-violating-election-law
32. https://thefederalist.com/2022/09/14/heres-how-big-tech-plans-to-rig-the-2022-midterms/
33. https://palaceintrigueblog.com/2018/12/20/the-uniparty-or-why-americans-are-destined-to-revolt/
34. https://youtu.be/Nyvxt1svxso, 3:15
35. https://freedomfirstnetwork.com/2022/07/the-rapid-rise-of-the-uniparty-swamp-and-how-to-stop-it
36. For an excellent 'quick read' summary of how Congress really works, see **The Confessions of Congressman X**, Congressman X and Robert Atkinson, Mill City Press (2016)
37. https://thehill.com/homenews/media/513902-cnn-ridiculed-for-fiery-but-mostly-peaceful-caption-with-video-of-burning/
38. https://www.westernjournal.com/mostly-peaceful-riots-soar-1b-damages-setting-new-record/
39. https://www.realclearpolitics.com/articles/2020/09/02/why_wont_biden_condemn_antifa_or_blm_violence_144118.html#!
40. https://nypost.com/2020/08/19/democrats-stay-silent-on-violence-in-their-cities-devine/
41. https://tennesseestar.com/2022/08/22/younger-americans-identify-as-independent-more-than-republicans-democrats-combined/
42. https://www.washingtonexaminer.com/news/federal-authorities-wont-say-why-armed-capitol-rioters-disappeared-from-fbis-most-wanted-list
43. https://www.washingtonexaminer.com/news/politics/ray-epps-january-6-riot-new-york-times
44. https://www.nationalreview.com/2017/07/john-mccains-obamacare-vote-was-indefensible/
45. https://amgreatness.com/2022/09/22/meme-them-mock-them/

5. 2024 Is Coming

1. Admittedly, the parable of the blind men and the elephant is more than a bit ironic, considering just how tightly the RINO Establishment clings to the elephant as the symbol of the GOP.
2. For more detailed insights into the nature of the DC Swamp, I highly recommend Rep. Ken Buck's ***Drain the Swamp***, ***The Confessions of Congressman X*** by Congressman X and Robert Atkinson, and the works of investigative reporter Peter Schweizer.
3. https://doccontrarian.substack.com/p/pitchfork-populism
4. https://www.washingtonpost.com/politics/2022/09/27/mccarthy-midterms-gop/
5. https://politicalwire.com/2023/01/03/mccarthy-moves-into-the-speakers-office-before-vote/
6. https://doccontrarian.substack.com/p/speaker-mccarthy-and-the-elephant
7. https://www.youtube.com/watch?v=RhL9iFkBaus at 6:07. The full transcript of President Trump's 2020 RNC acceptance speech can be read at https://www.theepochtimes.com/mkt_app/read-full-transcript-of-president-trumps-rnc-acceptance-speech_3479265.html
8. https://www.bbc.com/news/world-us-canada-48994931
9. https://www.theepochtimes.com/top-white-house-advisor-squad-wants-america-to-be-a-socialist-open-borders-country_3011606.html
10. https://nypost.com/2021/09/22/the-squads-anti-semites-carry-the-day-among-house-democrats-yet-again/
11. https://thehill.com/policy/energy-environment/426353-ocasio-cortez-the-world-will-end-in-12-years-if-we-dont-address/
12. https://hannity.com/media-room/mega-maga-half-the-people-at-last-five-trump-rallies-were-new-team-trump-says/
13. https://www.cnbc.com/2022/10/11/imf-cuts-global-growth-forecast-for-2023-warns-worst-is-yet-to-come.html
14. https://min.news/en/economy/59fd0fe0c81c95e887daad0e09cdbd55.html
15. https://www.trevorloudon.com/2022/10/bidens-energy-depression-is-nigh/
16. https://fortune.com/2022/08/30/steve-hanke-predicts-recession-whopper-2023-m2-money-supply-growth/
17. https://www.heritage.org/crime-and-justice/commentary/are-parents-being-tagged-domestic-terrorists-the-fbi-justice
18. https://reason.com/2021/10/06/ag-merrick-garland-fbi-critical-race-theory-parents-schools-domestic-terrorists/
19. Op. cit., #116, above
20. https://www.prlog.org/12934310-judge-allows-attorney-general-to-target-parents-as-domestic-terrorists-parents-vow-to-appeal.html
21. https://thefederalist.com/2021/10/06/across-america-parents-refuse-to-be-intimidated-by-bidens-attorney-general-labeling-them-domestic-terrorists/
22. https://www.youtube.com/watch?v=vxTMNu31DHU

23. https://www.washingtonexaminer.com/backpack-funding-puts-focus-on-students-not-school-districts

6. Maga: 2024 And Beyond

1. Transcript available at https://www.rev.com/blog/transcripts/former-president-donald-trump-speaks-at-cpac-8-06-22-transcript
2. https://www.theguardian.com/us-news/2017/feb/23/steve-bannon-cpac-donald-trump-media-campaign-pledges
3. https://www.newsmax.com/finance/georgementz/trump-economy-best-50/2019/06/05/id/919096/
4. https://www.eia.gov/todayinenergy/detail.php?id=43395
5. https://www.foxnews.com/opinion/hallmarks-biden-disaster-generation-newt-gingrich
6. Op. cit.
7. Transcript available at https://www.rev.com/blog/transcripts/former-president-donald-trump-speaks-at-cpac-8-06-22-transcript
8. Transcript available at https://www.rev.com/blog/transcripts/former-president-trump-announces-2024-presidential-bid-transcript
9. From the President's 2022 America First PAC Convention remarks, Op. cit.
10. From the President's CPAC 2022 remarks, Op. cit.
11. https://rumble.com/v2binw8-live-president-donald-trump-delivers-remarks-at-cpac.html

7. Moving Beyond Maga

1. https://www.dailymail.co.uk/news/article-11887357/Trump-releases-video-waits-indictment-vowing-dismantle-deep-state.html
2. https://www.theguardian.com/us-news/2017/feb/23/steve-bannon-cpac-donald-trump-media-campaign-pledges
3. Executive Order 13957, "Executive Order on Creating Schedule F In The Excepted Service", issued October 21, 2020. Full text at https://trumpwhitehouse.archives.gov/presidential-actions/executive-order-creating-schedule-f-excepted-service/
4. https://www.govexec.com/management/2021/01/biden-sign-executive-order-killing-schedule-f-restoring-collective-bargaining-rights/171569/
5. https://saraacarter.com/biden-undoes-five-of-trumps-key-executive-orders/
6. https://libertyunderfire.org/2022/09/fbi-doj-colluded-against-trump-in-elections-2016-2020-and-2022/
7. https://americanmind.org/memo/abolish-the-cia/
8. https://headlineusa.com/massie-float-idea-dissolve-fbi-doj/
9. https://www.gatestoneinstitute.org/17602/disband-the-fbi

10. https://amgreatness.com/2021/06/21/recent-history-suggests-fbi-involvement-in-january-6/
11. https://www.washingtontimes.com/news/2022/aug/11/time-to-dissolve-the-fbi/
12. https://www.youtube.com/watch?v=jKofnVkUwBA
13. https://www.thebalancemoney.com/simpson-bowles-plan-summary-history-would-it-work-3306323
14. https://www.crfb.org/blogs/five-years-simpson-bowles-how-much-it-have-we-enacted
15. https://www.youtube.com/watch?v=wDYNVH0U3cs
16. Thomas Sowell's 1996 classic **The Vision of the Anointed: Self-Congratulation as a Basis for Social Policy** goes into great detail about how feelings-driven, Elitist social policies are frequently divorced from reality, including their own costs and consequences. As a guide to understanding the 'how's and why's' behind Leftist's support for their taxpayer-funded social engineering, it is highly recommended reading.
17. https://ourfiniteworld.com/wp-content/uploads/2022/10/The-interconnection-of-energy-limits-and-the-economy-Final.pdf
18. ibid
19. https://justthenews.com/government/federal-agencies/fri-head-us-oil-and-gas-association-says-biden-admin-kneecapped
20. https://www.nationalreview.com/news/feds-discover-largest-oil-natural-gas-reserve-in-history/
21. https://www.youtube.com/watch?v=Dtf4Q_qzx44
22. https://wattsupwiththat.com/2018/03/08/clean-coal-carbon-capture-and-enhanced-oil-recovery-part-deux/
23. https://www.heartland.org/news-opinion/news/notes-from-frigid-texas-wind-and-solar-power-fail-when-you-need-them-the-most
24. https://futurism.com/the-byte/carbon-dioxide-trees-grow-faster
25. https://www.youtube.com/watch?v=TjlmFr4FMvI
26. https://www.theorganicprepper.com/solar-powered-items/
27. https://youtu.be/ehHibdfvSqM
28. https://thepremierdaily.com/radioactive-diamond-battery/
29. https://techxplore.com/news/2022-10-molten-salt-micro-nuclear-reactor-nuclear.html
30. https://www.zerohedge.com/weather/nothing-do-man-astrophysicist-says-climate-cultists-are-gravy-train-make-money
31. https://www.youtube.com/watch?v=_bDXXWQxK38&list=PLNJYKz9EBu5yppNSSfHDvvXwQOa1m7a22&index=9&t=1470s
32. https://www.naturalnews.com/2018-04-19-praise-for-the-proton-latest-battery-breakthrough-may-free-us-from-lithium-ion.html
33. https://www.theepochtimes.com/mkt_app/china-to-activate-experimental-nuclear-molten-salt-reactor-hopes-to-obtain-full-intellectual-rights_4673244.html
34. https://thefederal.com/science/thorium-india-nuclear-reactor-power-fuel/
35. https://www.ornl.gov/molten-salt-reactor/history

36. https://www.ornl.gov/molten-salt-reactor
37. https://www.energy.gov/ne/articles/nrc-approves-new-approach-streamline-advanced-reactor-licensing-process
38. https://singularityhub.com/2022/08/05/the-first-small-modular-nuclear-reactor-design-was-just-approved-by-us-regulators/
39. https://interestingengineering.com/innovation/groundbreaking-motionless-wind-turbine
40. https://www.theepochtimes.com/mkt_app/ex-treasury-secretary-blasts-hostile-fossil-fuel-policies-we-made-a-mistake_4786406.html
41. https://www.realclearpolitics.com/articles/2019/03/25/green_new_deal_is_same_old_socialist_con_game__139837.html#!
42. https://www.theepochtimes.com/exclusive-j6deleted-internet-sting-operation-exposes-in-real-time-how-twitter-manipulated-jan-6-narrative_4796503.html
43. https://townhall.com/tipsheet/katiepavlich/2022/06/07/january-6-committee-hired-a-tv-producer-to-make-their-hearings-more-dramatic-n2608335
44. https://www.upcounsel.com/legal-def-under-color-of-state-law
45. https://www.justice.gov/crt/deprivation-rights-under-color-law
46. https://www.cagw.org/media/press-releases/citizens-against-government-waste-releases-2022-congressional-pig-book
47. https://thefederalist.com/2020/09/15/trump-signs-historic-abraham-accords-for-peace-in-the-middle-east/
48. https://www.washingtontimes.com/news/2022/feb/28/trumps-abraham-accords-continue-to-rack-up-wins/
49. https://www.washingtonexaminer.com/policy/economy/nafta-replaced-trump-signs-usmca-trade-deal-with-canada-and-mexico
50. https://nypost.com/2021/06/13/bidens-illegal-immigration-welcome-mat-caused-border-crisis/
51. https://millermeeks.house.gov/media/in-the-news/conservative-alternative-biden-immigration-disaster
52. https://rightwingnews.com/democrats/ann-coulter-time-to-end-all-immigration-for-10-years/
53. https://www.numbersusa.com/content/nusablog/beckr/september-2-2009/ted-kennedys-immigration-legacy-and-why-did-he-do-it.html
54. Ibid, also see embedded links
55. https://www.youtube.com/watch?v=TQvB_YWkW10
56. https://www.youtube.com/watch?v=62sp1UeRvzw
57. https://www.termlimits.com/
58. https://www.youtube.com/watch?v=L_eRayyB2eo
59. https://www.youtube.com/watch?v=TnwGdl1YrQ8&t=3s
60. https://www.thebulwark.com/ten-proposals-on-how-to-really-drain-the-swamp/
61. https://youtu.be/8ZvimqX7Nuo
62. https://www.phrases.org.uk/meanings/may-you-live-in-interesting-times.html
63. https://www.businessinsider.com/dark-maga-explained-far-right-memes-calling-for-trump-revenge-2022-5

8. Bonus Chapter—The Sins Of Trump And The Big Steal

1. A quick introduction to the forces 'behind the curtain' by Mark Dice is at https://www.youtube.com/watch?v=ei_EI3wVSQ
2. https://www.westernjournal.com/poll-majority-likely-voters-now-believe-cheating-impacted-results-2020-election/, pub. June 11, 2021
3. https://bannonswarroom.com/wp-content/uploads/2020/12/The-Immaculate-Deception-12.15.20-1.pdf
4. SARCASM!!!

9. Afterward—The Red Speech

1. https://www.whitehouse.gov/briefing-room/speeches-remarks/2022/09/01/remarks-by-president-bidenon-the-continued-battle-for-the-soul-of-the-nation/
2. https://altoday.com/archives/47103-bill-chitwood-a-maga-call-to-action-following-joe-bidens-red-speech